Lith. & Print by W. Boell 311 Walnut St. Phil.

Lith. & Print. of W. Boell 311 Walnut St. Phil.

A
PRACTICAL TREATISE
ON
STREET OR HORSE-POWER RAILWAYS:
THEIR
Location, Construction and Management;
WITH
GENERAL PLANS AND RULES
FOR THEIR
ORGANIZATION AND OPERATION;
TOGETHER WITH
EXAMINATIONS AS TO THEIR COMPARATIVE ADVANTAGES OVER THE
OMNIBUS SYSTEM;
AND
INQUIRIES AS TO THEIR VALUE FOR INVESTMENT;
INCLUDING COPIES OF
MUNICIPAL ORDINANCES RELATING THERETO.

By ALEXANDER EASTON, C. E.
PHILADELPHIA.

PHILADELPHIA:
CRISSY & MARKLEY, PRINTERS, GOLDSMITHS HALL, LIBRARY STREET.
1859.

TO

SAMUEL J. REEVES, ESQUIRE,

OF

PHILADELPHIA,

THIS WORK IS RESPECTFULLY DEDICATED AS A MARK

OF

FRIENDSHIP AND ESTEEM.

PHILADELPHIA, FEBRUARY, 1859.

INTRODUCTION.

Having received numerous enquiries from various parts of the United States and Europe, in relation to the construction and general operation of Street Railways, I have been induced to publish the following pages, which I trust will be found practically useful to the Engineer, Contractor, Shareholder, and Director of Street Railways, as well as to the Authorities of those Cities whose streets are about to be occupied by them.

I have been compelled to omit estimates of cost of construction, as the price of materials varies in different localities; this, however, with Engineers, will be but a simple work of calculation.

I have endeavored to confine myself as much as possible to such *practical* information as, during my own experience in the construction of works of this nature, I have considered most important, and in this effort I have been materially aided by the kind advice of my friend, Strickland Kneass, Esq., whose authority in such matters is undisputed.

I also take great pleasure in acknowledging the kindness of L. M. Stevens, Esq., Accountant of The Union Railway, Boston, for much general statistics and information in the department of which he is so efficient an officer.

The following, I hope, will be the means of inciting investigation to a system which, although now in its infancy, is rapidly providing a secure and profitable investment for a large amount of capital.

ALEXANDER EASTON.

Philadelphia,
402 Walnut Street.

A PRACTICAL TREATISE

ON

STREET OR HORSE-POWER RAILWAYS.

CHAPTER I.

Popular prejudice is the great enemy with which the advocates of innovation have had to combat, and strange as it may appear, it is nevertheless practically true, that the more useful the measure advocated, the greater has been the amount of opposition brought to bear against it, even by parties who have subsequently been benefited by the very measures they sought to defeat.

A glance at the early history of turnpike roads will clearly show the difficulties encountered by their projectors—but which, when overcome, became the favored improvement of the age, and legislative halls sounded with angry debate for their protection, so soon as railroads were proposed, denouncing them as a nuisance, and their corporators as visionary speculators. So it was with the introduction of canals, steamboats, and even gas, the arguments against which, brought forward by the opposition having, in each instance, exhibited the grossest ignorance of science, and of the practical effect of the proposed improvements, all of which is applicable at the present day, and has been experienced by those who proposed the introduction of street railways.

The interest which operated against turnpike roads was that of the muleteer; the interest which operated against railroads was that of stage coach and wagon proprietors, and in the case of street railways the opposition is from omnibus companies and antiquated stage communities, whose palpable interest it is to defeat a measure, which invades their imagined rights, by the substitution of a means of communication so manifestly useful and necessary, as to completely destroy the system to which they are so faithfully wedded. They use the means employed in their interests to influence, and lead on opposition, until having obtained certain provisoes in the charter for their *especial* benefit; the time has arrived to fraternize with the enemy—when they at once become strong advocates for street railways; and unfortunately, without the influence to quench the flame of prejudice which they have ignited.

If any better means than the railway can be devised, which will more effectually obviate existing evils and accomplish the objects desired, let it be introduced: but the street railways have been tested in the cities of New York, Boston, and Philadelphia, and are found to be the "improvement of the age," being so successful in their operations, as to excite the surprise of their most sanguine projectors, and the admiration of the community at large.

That increased facilities for commerce and transportation cause greater influx of traffic and travel to the principal streets of large cities, is indisputably recognized, and where the consequent inconvenience of narrow thoroughfares cannot be corrected, it must be modified by economizing time and space.

Time is economized by regularity of transit; the cars being quickly stopped by the application of the brake, the most refractory horses are immediately arrested; while the whole operation becomes so mechanical, that the horses, when accustomed to the signals of the bell, stop or start without any action on the part of the driver, by which means a time table can be effectively used, and business men are not subjected to delays incident to the old,—and we trust soon to say obsolete—*omnibus system.*

Space is economized, because omnibuses, (the most numerous and dangerous portion of the travel,) surging from side to side of the streets, are abolished, while the work heretofore inadequately performed by three of those vehicles, is easily accomplished by one car, in half the time, notwithstanding it is concentrated and confined to one channel.

By the convenience afforded the public by the cars, the sidewalks are relieved from pedestrians, and the centre of the street from vehicles; a seat can be taken and vacated without trouble or danger to the occupants of the car, whether invalid or infirm, and the rails present such an even and smooth surface for the wheels of ordinary vehicles, that the drivers avail themselves of their continued use. It is a most difficult matter to dispel from the ignorant or prejudiced mind, the idea, that the railway will be constantly occupied by continuous trains of cars, which beyond a doubt would block up the street, obstruct the travel, and be a most confirmed nuisance, ruinous to the locality; whereas in reality the rails themselves form no obstruction, but rather invite vehicles on the track; the passage of the little car is momentary, as it moves quietly along the street; and the nuisance occasioned by the rattling of omnibuses over the rough stones is abolished, leaving the streets nearly as noiseless as when covered with snow; the advantages of the smooth rail, are thus neither few nor unimportant. Any one, familiar with the laws of momentum, can readily understand the effect of the constant jar to buildings, occasioned by the passage of omnibuses, and particularly in the thronged thoroughfares, where buildings are most elevated.

If, however, the solidity of construction should prevent injurious results, there are many minor disturbances, —if not so dangerous, almost as annoying—which cannot be prevented, such as the constant vibration of pier-glasses, gas pipes, &c., (as occasional showers of white flakes, and plaster fragments attest,) without enumerating the very serious annoyance to the invalid.

The great reduction of friction on the car, and the smoothness of the rail, obviate all these evil effects by removing the cause.

Here is a picture.—A wet day,—every corner of the side walk crowded with impatient pedestrians, each one anxiously peering up or down the street in search of the particular omnibus among the fifteen or twenty approaching, to carry him home, which with as many more coming in the opposite direction, so effectually choke up the street, that the drays and carts unable to cross at the intersections, render the highway impassable to private vehicles, and are therefore driven to other streets, avoiding danger and delay; the omnibuses crowded to excess, cannot accommodate the vexed crowd on the side-walk, and the sudden halt with imminent risk of collision, with the drivers' "plenty of room, sir," with twenty inside—by no means softens the temper either of those in waiting, or those, who seated—not comfortably—look upon each moment of unnecessary delay, as an infringement on their rights.

Here is another.—Not an *omnibus* is seen in the whole length of the street—carriages, drays and carts move with comparative ease, little strips of iron are laid along the street, upon and across which, vehicles pass without inconvenience, and which, the drivers (particularly of private carriages) evidently seek; there is no crowd, for the little cars glide along rapidly and frequently, accommodating every body; at a slight signal the bell rings, the horses stop, the passenger is comfortably seated, no rain drops in from the roof, the conductor is always ready to take the fare when offered, and the echo, "great improvement, this," is constantly repeated.

There is no accident on record, of injury to any passenger of street railways, whilst occupying a seat in the car; some few have happened to boys and incautious persons, from drunkenness, jumping from the cars whilst in motion, &c., but even these, are few in comparison with omnibus accidents.

The acquisition of a suburban railway on turnpikes, or public roads, is perhaps, a greater benefit to the farmer, than to any other portion of the community: the desideratum in constructing the surface of all roads, is to diminish friction, to this end, roads have been macadamized, planked, and a variety of other means have been resorted to, but none have so effectually accomplished the object and improved the facilities for traveling in nearly all seasons, as the smooth iron rail: and when common roads are impassable, even to light vehicles, the farmer, using the rails, can double his load in going to market, whilst those not enjoying its advantages, are either prevented leaving home, or subjected to use a road almost impassable, and ruinous to horses, even with a lighter load than would justify transportation.

The benefit of the railway may be estimated, by actual observation of lines now constructed on plank roads; for whilst that side covered with good plank, is almost deserted, the railway is used by vehicles of every description; it can be appreciated, not only by those who drive fast horses, but by the invalid who enjoys a ride free from jolting, and the teamster whose pride is the condition of his animals, but by none so forcibly, as the horse, whose loads though increased in weight require but a minimum of tractive power.

Prejudice, is the great enemy to overcome, to make the system of street railroads universally popular, and to such as object to them, the following paragraph, extracted from a Philadelphia paper, is respectfully recommended:

"THE OMNIBUS vs. THE CITY RAILROADS.

" Since the progressionists have made it fashionable to turn all our streets into railroads, and to cry down the omnibus, I wish to say a word in behalf of the latter.

" It will, I hope, be a long while before the citizens of

Philadelphia will be contented to endure such a nuisance as the railroad is likely to be. Look at the Third street, the Market street, the Broad street, and the Willow street railroads. Are they not unmitigated nuisances? Every body knows they are, and yet a set of speculators would make all the streets in the city just like these, to the inconvenience of the public, and to the damage of property.

"What is the use of experience, if we go directly counter to the lessons it teaches? Who would believe that any set of men could be found, so desperate, and so defiant of the sense of the public on this question, as to insist upon laying a railroad in two of the best streets in the city, viz.: Chestnut and Walnut streets?

"Yet it is so. A charter has actually been granted to a company to perpetrate this great outrage, and it is likely to be accomplished, unless the people speak out.

"I am an omnibus man, and am opposed to railroads; and while I am content to remedy any defects of the present omnibus system, I protest against their being driven out of the streets.

"Let us consider what are the objections to the omnibus, and suggest the remedy. It is said, and the charge, I confess, has some weight, that, in Chestnut street particularly, they occupy the entire street, lumbering about, careless of all other vehicles, first on one side, then on the other, so that it is dangerous to attempt to drive a private carriage through the street at all. Let us learn wisdom of our enemies. It would be certainly desirable, if practicable, to compel all the omnibus drivers—a very reliable and compliant set of men—to keep their unwieldy machines exactly in the middle of the street, imitating in this respect the railroad. If this were done, then every body would know how to pass them. Fast young men and tigers could show their skill in driving their light wagons within an inch of the omnibus, on a full trot, without danger of being crushed, as now, by a lee-lurch of the great battering ram. To insure this end, I would pass an ordinance, and impose a fine upon every Jehu that did not comply with the rule.

"It may be objected that the drivers could not, if they would, keep the exact middle line of the street. I am ready to meet this objection. Take two metal bars, nearly flat, and lay them at a proper distance apart, so that the wheels could travel on them; the horses would naturally keep between them. This would have the effect, also, of diminishing the terrible noise the vehicle now makes over the rough stones. To prevent the wheels running off the metal bars or slabs, a slight projection might be made on each, say about seven-eighths of an inch high, and, if you please, let the wheels have a corresponding rim on their tires. This device, as any one may see, would effectually prevent the omnibus from wabbling from curve to curve, and surging through holes, and over loose stones.

"It is evident, too, that, owing to the ease with which great weights may be pulled over smooth surfaces, a desirable modification of the present 'bus may be made. The wheels can be much smaller, and the frame let down lower, so that feeble persons and children may be able to use this mode of conveyance, to which they have hitherto been almost debarred, owing to the difficulty of ascent to the back door. The omnibus could also be much enlarged, without increasing its weight—thus affording room for a greater number of passengers—a very important matter in a hot summer day, and when it is raining.

"I think I discover a smile on the lips of the scorner of my proposed improvement, inasmuch as I have provided for the omnibus keeping the exact centre of the street, but not for their passing each other in opposite directions. I anticipate the sneering criticism, and have the remedy at hand. I am not ashamed to avail myself of a good idea, although it comes from the enemy. Let all the omnibuses run up Chestnut street and down Walnut, or vice versa, completing the circuit by using the cross streets at either end. The system will then be complete; and with this improvement easily brought about, I defy the opponents of the omnibus to point out a single remaining objection. Why then insist upon having railroads, when it is well known there are so many respectable people opposed to them, so that the very name is detestable. Witness the immense list of remonstrances against the Chestnut and Walnut street Company laying rails in those streets. The improved omnibus system will satisfy the entire community. Nine out of ten of these remonstrants will, if they have the opportunity, petition Councils to adopt my plan, in the place of the horrid railroad. No one will be silly enough to assert that this system will injure the property of those living on the streets where it is introduced; on the contrary, it will enhance the value of it. All complaints against the old rudderless monster—as I once heard a malicious railroad man call that highly respectable public vehicle, the omnibus—will be at an end; and it will hardly be recognized by its old admirers, in its improved shape and parts.

"Again, the railroad in the hands of a company is a perfect nonopoly; and, although their advocates boast that they help the income of the city treasury, and diminish the taxes, by keeping the streets in good repair at their own expense, yet the people very properly object to monopolies.

"Now, there is no reason why a revenue of the same sort, and a stipulation to keep the streets in order, may not be equally well secured under my proposed new omnibus system. Charge twenty-five dollars per annum for the privilege for each omnibus, and compel the owners to keep the streets in order.

"This could not, perhaps, be done, without concert of action between the several owners; but to insure its being carried out, I would suggest that a number of individuals club together, and take certain streets, and that Councils recognize the club, and hold them jointly responsible. This would be a very different concern from an incorporated company. The former consists of individual citizens; the latter is a monopoly, and have the right, by an act of the Legislature, to use a great seal.

"Of course, the railroad advocates will find, or try to invent, some objections to my plan; but I appeal to every reflecting man, if it does not possess all the merits claimed for the railroad, and at the same time preserve all the good characteristics of the omnibus, with none of its disadvantages.

"Gentlemen in their private carriages may then have some satisfaction in driving through Chestnut street. There will be no more noise, no blockading the street; people may converse and read newspapers in the omnibus; ladies' dresses will not be splashed with dirty water from the gutters; the street will be inviting; shopping will be pleasant pastime, and every body will be pleased with the change.

"Thus, I have proved that we can do without the railroad. Some one may say, 'a rose by any other name will smell as sweet;' but people will have their fancies, their notions, or, if you please, their prejudices. Let no one do unnecessary violence to them. If my improved omnibus system will answer, and satisfy both parties, why insist upon having a railroad? Let the streets be used for what they were intended for.

"OMNIBUS."

CHAPTER II.

In entering upon the question "does the stock of street railways afford a secure and profitable investment?" it is necessary to lay before the reader some of the many reasons why the larger proportion of railroads, are not remunerative to the stockholders—and it would be found if the accounts and transactions of the majority of bankrupt railroad companies were examined, that if judiciously located as to termini, the fault has not arisen so much from a lack of income, but because that income has been injudiciously expended; and that the cost of construction has not been proportioned to a fair estimate of the prospective business; in the natural desire to secure the construction of the work, estimates have been furnished, undervaluing the cost and overrating the anticipated profits, thus requiring of necessity a resort to loans at usurious rates for construction alone, leaving the equipment to be scantily provided for by a floating debt, or some other financial operation: yet, however much the system may be condemned, there is that tendency to speculation, in the principle upon which such enterprises are conducted, that examples will ever be disregarded, and works will continue to be constructed with such mismanagement, as can but result disastrously to stockholders—the law which must govern the value of a railroad, as well as every other undertaking, for investment, is that it shall yield a profit equal to a fair interest on the whole amount of its cost.

Therefore in the construction of street railroads, let care be taken that the whole capital invested be judiciously and legitimately disbursed for the construction and equipment of the road, and that not too much money or credit be absorbed for such plunder, as lobbying bills—let the affairs of the company be, so far as possible, secure from imposition and mismanagement, by the appointment of *competent*, efficient and *respectable* officers, then, no doubt need exist that the permanent business of any thoroughfare which, if it had but barely maintained a line of omnibuses, will be amply remunerative to a railway company, and for these reasons: that the cost of transportation, including wear and tear of horses and cars and repairs of railway, is much less in proportion to the capacity, than that of omnibuses, whilst the increase of business induced by such strong additional facilities, is as ten to one, or, where one person traveled by the omnibus, ten travel in the car, either from necessity, luxury, convenience or speed, and this is the lowest estimate which the comparison of omnibus and railway statistics will allow.

One great advantage of the locations of most of the roads so far constructed in Philadelphia is, that they occupy the ground, and receive the traffic previously appropriated to *two* lines of omnibuses, both of which were in successful operation, which, with the increase of travel consequent upon the improved accommodations, before alluded to—must yield a large revenue, and is a strong argument in favor of the plan adopted, in preference to a double track on any one street, unless governed by advantages peculiar to itself.

Taking the statistics of cost, expenses and receipts of four street railways in New York and four street railways in Boston, which may be assumed to be a fair average on the whole, the cost of construction and equipment amounts to $5,044,520; the receipts for one year, $1,958,119; expenses for one year, including estimated wear and tear of stock and repairs of roadway, $1,319,208; being an income of $638,911, on a capital of $5,044,520, giving the cost of working at 67 per cent. of the total receipts. No returns have yet been made of the operations of the many railways laid down in Philadelphia, but from actual observation, it is calculated that the aggregate of their incomes will, in proportion to the amount invested, far exceed that of Boston and New York. The Citizens' Passenger Railway, on Tenth and Eleventh streets, which was considered the most desperate of all undertakings, (and would never have been constructed, but that it had for its leader and main support a gentleman whose fame and authority in railroad matters is unquestionable) has declared a dividend of 8½ per cent. in 5 months. The Philadelphia and Darby Passenger Railway, a suburban road constructed on a plank road, (with heavy grades and other disadvantages) is just completed, and five cars are insufficient to accommodate the permanent travel originally performed by one omnibus. The stockholders of this company have declined to entertain a proposal wherein an offer was made to lease the road for five years, keeping the same in repair, and paying a rent equal to eight per cent. per annum on the cost of construction.

The success of street railways in Philadelphia has induced property owners and capitalists to apply for charters of many others, of the ultimate success of some of which there is doubt: the introduction of so many lines will have the effect of reducing the management of the business to a more complete and economical system.

It is proposed to build a railway in New Jersey, from Camden to Haddonfield, a pleasant and quiet resort, much frequented during the summer season. Its prospects of business are very flattering. The corporators have already received a proposition to lease the road for a term of ten years, at a rental equal to six per cent. per annum, the lessee to keep the road in repair.

A steady increase of business has been experienced on all the lines, attributable partly to economy in management, but mainly to increased travel as the extremities of the streets become more densely populated.

The rapid increase of population about the depots, which are generally on the suburbs of the city, adds largely to the permanent business of the roads, and is the means of bringing into market, property which otherwise may have remained unsold and unimproved for years. Moreover, in times of panic, whilst most branches of industry have been paralysed, the business of street railways has been continued without interruption, with steadily increasing receipts, additional facilities for the conveyance of passengers, and a corresponding increase of the number of employees at the time when the curtailment of other enterprises was swelling the ranks of the unemployed.

Real estate along the lines of street railways has enhanced in value, handsome structures have taken the place of small dwellings, producing an increased rental, whilst the streets, being kept in repair by the railway company, and their property yielding an additional revenue to the city, the public is relieved of a large amount of taxation.

The following shows the increasing receipts for passenger fares on some of the railways in New York:

	1856.	1857.
Third Avenue Railroad, N. Y.,	$356,594 14	$405,278 95
Eighth Avenue Railroad, N. Y.,	304,864 98	341,471 63
Brooklyn City Railroad, N. Y.,	327,629 21	378,791 16
Sixth Avenue Railroad, N. Y.,	247,005 52	267,485 38

Comparative Monthly Receipts for Passenger Fares on Sixth Avenue Railroad.

	1855.	1856.	1857.
February,	$13,949 14	$17,545 43	$18,530 41
March,	16,628 73	20,049 51	20,812 74
April,	18,066 40	20,613 26	21,872 36
May,	19,101 11	21,099 24	23,433 20
June,	18,534 36	20,129 97	22,565 10
July,	18,270 13	19,343 73	21,345 24
August,	17,604 71	19,083 50	21,056 76
September,	19,788 08	21,965 19	25,261 40
October,	24,954 53	27,498 90	27,369 18
November,	21,111 53	21,833 71	22,128 94
December,	18,354 94	19,964 72	21,112 16
January, 1855,	13,604 56	17,878 36	21,997 89
Totals,	$219,968 22	$247,005 52	$267,485 38

It is impossible to furnish a general estimate of the travel on the route of a projected railway, as this will be influenced by local circumstances; the current expenses will be, as the number of cars employed; the profits should be in proportion thereto. The following statistics embrace all the information necessary to base the calculations of expenses:

SIXTH AVENUE RAILROAD, N. Y.

Within the past three years this company has added more than one hundred thousand dollars of property and valuable appliances to its assets, besides having paid off $12,000 of indebtedness at the time they took charge of the road, without interfering with the payments of dividends or incurring obligations; and the market value of its stock has risen from about 35 per cent. to par.

An increased number of horses and mules, and additional cars, have been indispensable to the accommodation of the increased business of the road.

COST OF ROAD AND EQUIPMENT.

For graduation and masonry, including pavement account in streets; for bridges; superstructure, including iron, - - - - - - -	$555,012 62
Passenger stations, buildings and fixtures; car-houses, machine shops, machinery and fixtures; land, land damages and fences, - - -	166,915 73
Passenger cars, - - - - - - -	61,101 76
Horses, mules and other motive power, including harness, - - - - - - -	71,927 11
Total cost of road and equipment, - - -	$854,957 22

RECEIPTS FOR ONE YEAR.

PASSENGER FARES, - - - -		$267,485 38
REAL ESTATE.		
Interest on mortgages held by the Company to November 1, -	$388 50	
Rent—Vesey, Barclay, and Forty-fourth street Houses, - -	639 80	
		1,028 30
TO WORKING THE ROAD IN GENERAL.		
One-half rent 56 Barclay street, paid by Eighth Avenue Railroad Company, - - - - -	1,000 00	
Damage to cars, fines, glass broken, &c., - - - - - - -	89 63	
Amounts carried forward,	$1,089 63	$268,513 68

Amounts brought forward,	$1,089 63	$268,513 68
Advertising in cars, $224; selling papers, $24, - - -	248 00	
Sundries, - - - -	17 23	
		1,354 86
To WORKING THE ROAD WITH MOTIVE POWER.		
Manure to Nov. 1, $1,000; difference in trades, $130, - -	$1,130 00	
24 horses, $1,919 50; 11 mules, $1,370, - - - - -	3,289 50	
Feed, wood, harness, old iron, &c.,	878 51	
Keeping horses, $83 44; set of harness, $30, - - - -	113 44	
Bill of plumbing, $5 22; shoeing horses, $8, - - - -	13 22	
		5,424 67
Premium on Spanish silver sold at the Mint, - - - -		129 80
Total receipts, - - - -		$275,423 01

EXPENSES.

To WORKING THE ROAD IN GENERAL.	
Services—Superintendent, $3,500; Deputy, $1,200, - - -	$4,700 00
Conductors, $21,200 65; Drivers, $28,038 44, - - -	49,239 09
Painters, blacksmiths, watchmen, starters, switchmen, carpenters, car-cleaners, and lamp-cleaner,	12,293 19
Taxes, $4,112 99; insurance, $2,145 06; car bodies, $2,946 99,	9,205 04
Receivers, $1,825; rent 56 Barclay street, $2,000, - - -	3,825 00
Amount carried forward,	$79,262 32

Amount brought forward,	$79,262 32	
Fluid, $713 61; oil, $498 86; car wheels, $3,211 75, - -	4,424 22	
Sundries—lumber, paint, glass, car lamps, brakes, pedestals, brass boxes, oil boxes, rubber springs, hardware, car mats, sprinkling streets, &c., &c., - - -	6,382 59	
		90,069 13
TO WORKING THE ROAD WITH MOTIVE POWER.		
Labor—Hostlers, $17,452 31; Harnessmaker, $728, - -	$18,180 31	
Blacksmiths, $5,844 74; iron, $1,850 36, - - - -	7,695 10	
Corn, $17,423 73; hay, $5,995 13; straw, $1,435 96, - -	24,854 82	
Oats, $8,947 20; corn meal, $69 86; gas, $715 66, - - -	9,732 72	
Horse nails, $51 52; leather and hardware, $720 58, - -	772 10	
Horses and mules, $11,351 50; horse medicine, $163 76, -	11,515 26	
Croton tax, $388 70; lumber, $199 85, - - - -	588 55	
Sundries—coal, sawdust, lime, tar, bags, currycombs, brushes, bells, brooms, &c., &c., - - -	1,728 27	
		75,067 13
TO REPAIRING THE TRACK, - -		4,646 11
TO EXTENDING THE TRACK		
On Vesey street, Sixth Avenue and Forty-third street, - -		9,277 11
TO REAL ESTATE.		
Additions to depot, new workshop, &c., - - - - - -	$4,389 18	
Amounts carried forward,	$4,389 18	$179,059 48

Amounts brought forward,	$4,389 18	$179,059 48
Interest on mortgages, - -	1,235 16	
Mortgage B. W. Bonney, Trustee, paid off, Oct. 19, - - -	3,000 00	
Labor on tunnel, - - -	247 83	
Rent of house in Forty-fourth st.,	356 25	
Searches, $6; plumbing, $49 29,	55 29	
Tinning cupola, $42 50; fencing Forty-third street, $18 77, -	61 27	
Flagging lots on Forty-fifth street, $44; repairs, Forty-fourth st., $2 25, - - - -	46 25	
		9,391 23
To EXPENSE.		
Salaries for 1857—President, Secretary, Treasurer and Clerk, -	$7,225 00	
Balance of salaries, 1856, - -	200 00	
Legal expenses and damages, -	1,211 21	
Special services and sundries, -	110 60	
		8,746 81
		$197,197 52
Balance applicable to dividends, - - -		$78,225 49

Length of double track, including sidings, 4⅜ miles.
Number of cars, 64.
Number of horses 166, and 188 mules—354.
Miles run by passenger cars, 950,572, in one year.
Number of passengers carried, 5,240,978 in one year.
Average cost of carrying each passenger, 3¾ cents.
Average expense of each car, $3,081, in one year
Average cost per mile run, 20¾ cents.
Average rate of speed, including stops, 4½ miles per hour.
Average rate of speed, in motion, 6 miles.
Rate of fare for passengers, 5 cents.

BROOKLYN CITY RAILROAD, N. Y.

Cost of Road and Equipment.

For bridges, - - - - -	$3,107 02	
Superstructure, including iron, -	573,063 49	
Stables and car houses, machine shops, machinery and fixtures, including land, - - - - - -	160,017 24	
Land damages, - - - - -	80 00	
Passenger cars, - - - -	85,802 75	
Engineering, - - - -	4,651 15	
Horses, mules, harness, &c., -	135,502 37	
Real estate, houses and lots, -	7,167 84	
Stages, sleighs, and miscellaneous articles, - - - - -	57,318 12	
		$1,026,709 98

Receipts for one year.

From passengers, - - - -	$378,791 16	
From other sources, as follows, viz:		
Interest, - - - - - -	2,160 38	
Rent, - - - - - -	1,606 15	
Manure, - - - - - -	3,345 87	
Cards, and selling papers, - -	1,344 07	
Old iron sold, - - - - -	537 98	
Wood, &c., - - - - -	92 37	
Feed, (part burned,) - - -	732 26	
		$388,610 24

Expenses of operating and maintaining road.

Repairs roadway, buildings, &c., -	3,566 44	
Office expenses, stationery, &c., -	337 15	
Office rent, - - - - -	1,000 00	
Clerks and receivers, - - -	2,569 50	
Amounts carried forward,	$7,473 09	$388,610 24

Amounts brought forward,	$7,473 09	$388,610 24
Foremen of stables, starters, watchmen and switch tenders, stablemen, turn-table men, conductors, and drivers, - - - - - -	127,913 48	
Hay and feed, - - - -	77,105 07	
Fuel, cost and labor of preparing for use, - - - - - -	1,099 47	
Horses replenished, - - -	13,869 60	
Horse shoeing, - - - -	11,230 95	
Oil and waste for passenger cars,	576 40	
Repairing cars, wheels, &c., -	10,422 75	
Damage for injuries of persons, -	222 00	
Damage to property, - - -	146 92	
General superintendence, - -	3,250 00	
Contingencies not enumerated, including taxes on personal property, insurance, licenses, &c., &c., -	34,523 24	
For interest, - - - -	1,587 63	
		289,420 60
Balance applicable to dividends,		$99,189 64

Length of double track, including sidings, 20 miles.
Number of cars, 100.
Miles run by cars, 1,891,215, in one year.
Number of passengers carried, 7,575,823, in one year.
Average cost of carrying each passenger, 3¾ cents.
Average expense of each car, $2,894, in one year.
Average cost per mile run, 15⅓ cents.
Rate of fare, 5 cents.

THIRD AVENUE RAILROAD, N. Y.

This road was bought from a private partnership for $1,170,000.

The original proprietors of the road are supposed to have bought out five lines of omnibuses, at a cost of about $400,000. The present officers were connected with the road for the first time in November, 1854, and found no books or accounts for previous operations and expenses incurred under the former management.

There is no construction or equipment account. All expenses are charged to the operations of the road.

Estimated value of the property of the Company.

Roadway and track complete, - - -	$1,000,000 00
Real estate, - - - - - - -	40,000 00
Horses and mules, - - - - -	77,000 00
Harness, &c., - - - - - -	3,000 00
Cars, &c., - - - - - - -	50,000 00
	$1,170,000 00

Earnings from passengers for one year, - -	$405,278 95
Cash on hand, - - - - - - -	50,527 21
Receipts from manure, sale of old material, and other sources, - - - - - -	13,750 95
Total, - - - - - - -	$469,557 11

FOR TRANSPORTATION EXPENSES, VIZ:

Expenses of operating road.

Harness, - - -	$1,892 57	
Repairs of passenger cars,	10,449 21	
Painting, - - -	2,058 43	
Hardware and lumber, -	1,147 74	
Incidental (snow) expenses,	1,014 28	
Law expenses, - -	1,137 94	
Amounts carried forward,	$17,700 17	$469,557 11

Am'ts brought forward,	$17,700 17		$469,557 11
Office expenses, stationery, rents, &c., - -	5,032 48		
Conductors and drivers,	70,962 76		
Meal and hay, - -	68,899 05		
Pay roll, - - -	49,969 60		
Horses, - - -	20,480 56		
Salaries, - - -	11,764 16		
Insurance, - - -	1,352 60		
Fuel, - - - -	448 37		
Oil, - - - -	1,347 22		
Fluid and gas, - -	1,932 83		
Damages, injuries of persons,	852 75		
General expenses of stable,	566 53		
Contingencies, - -	1,547 23		
		$252,856 31	
Expenses of maintaining the road, or real estate of the Corporation.			
Track expense, - -	$5,453 05		
Paving, - - -	1,865 69		
Cost of iron used in repairs,	3,339 34		
Repairs of buildings, -	170 63		
		10,828 71	
Real estate, - - - - -		68,673 64	
Interest, - - - - -		3,500 00	
Taxes, - - - - -		3,402 48	
Equipment, &c., - - - -		6,250 00	
Payments to sewer account, - -		2,400 00	
Loss, Suffolk Bank, - - -		3,756 93	
			351,668 07
Net profits, - - -			117,889 04
To payment of dividend of 8 pr ct. on cost of construction and equipment,		$93,600 00	
Surplus cash on hand, - - -		24,289 04	
			$117,889 04

Length of double track, including sidings, 6 miles.
Number of cars, 71, and 12 stages.
Number of horses, 563, and 7 mules.
Number of passengers carried during the year, 8,105,515.
Average cost of carrying each passenger, 4⅓ cents.
Average rate of speed, 6 miles per hour.

CAMBRIDGE RAILROAD, BOSTON.

This railroad, constructed in the streets of Boston and Cambridge, from Bowdoin Square, in Boston, to Harvard Square, in Cambridge; and from thence to Mount Auburn Cemetery and the line between Cambridge and Watertown, where it connects with the Waltham and Watertown Railroad; with a Branch from Harvard Square, in Cambridge, through North Avenue. The construction of the road was commenced September 1, 1855, and it was so far completed, March 26, 1856, that cars were run upon it on that day, on experimental trips, for the first time, by the Union Railway Company, to whom it has been leased.

This was the first horse railway built in New England, and its originators experienced considerable difficulty in obtaining subscriptions to the stock and bonds of the Company, to pay for the construction of the road, owing to the fact that the experiment of a horse railroad was one at that time untried, and its success doubted. Such great doubt was manifested as to the success of this road, that the Company could with difficulty secure a subscription to their stock and bonds to the amount of about $43,000 only. The contractor, therefore, agreed to receive this amount on account of his contract; the balance to be paid him in stock and bonds. By the original terms of subscription each subscriber had the right to take either stock or bonds for the amount of his subscription, as he might choose; and even then, so little faith had the subscribers, in the success of the project, that of the $43,000 paid in, in cash, $37,000 was taken in bonds, and only about $6,000 in stock; the bonds being secured by a mortgage and a sinking fund, and drawing interest, and therefore considered preferable to stock—the dividends on which, were then considered *doubtful*. The bonds *now* draw interest at six per cent., while the stock draws a regular dividend of nine per cent.*

The Company now own a finished road, equal in length to nearly ten and a half miles of single track, which has cost $316,777 14, including the $33,000 paid for bridge tolls. They have no floating debt, and the funded debt, $150,000, will not be due for over twenty-three years, when there will be a sinking fund for its payment. All claims and demands against the Company have been settled, and their accounts have been all closed. The interest on their bonds, the percentage for the sinking fund for the payment thereof, and the dividend of nine per cent. on their stock have, without a single exception, been promptly paid. No further issues of stock or bonds are anticipated, unless some extensions of the road be built—which cannot be done by this Company alone, but only at the request of the Union Railway Company, who, in case of any such extension, are bound to equip and run the extension, and are bound to pay to the holders of any stock or

* This is entirely distinct from what has been paid by the Union Railway Company to their own stockholders as the profits of operating the road.

bonds issued to pay therefor, the interest and the dividends now paid to the original stock and bondholders of this Company, together with the same percentage on the bonds as is now paid on those already issued, for their redemption at maturity.

The Union Railway Company, (Boston,) was incorporated in 1855, with authority to lease the Cambridge Railroad and any other connecting road. In pursuance of this authority the Company has leased the Cambridge Railroad and the Waltham and Watertown Railroad. The Cambridge Railroad is leased to this Company for the term of fifty years from the date of the approval of the act incorporating the Cambridge Railroad Company, May 25, 1853; this Company agreeing to furnish all the equipment necessary for running the road, to keep the road in repair during the continuance of the lease, to pay all taxes assessed thereon during that time, and to pay as rent therefor the following sums:

To the Stockholders of the Cambridge Railroad Company 4½ per cent. semi-annually, (April 1st and October 1st,) on their 1,600 shares of stock; amounting, per annum, to - - - - - - - -	$14,400 00
To the Bondholders of the Cambridge Railroad Company the interest due semi-annually, (January 1st and July 1st,) on the $150,000 of Mortgage Bonds issued by said Company; amounting, per annum, to - -	9,000 00
And to the Trustees of the Sinking Fund, for the redemption of the said Mortgage Bonds at maturity, one per cent., semi-annually, (April 1st and October 1st,) on the amount thereof; amounting, per annum, to -	3,000 00
Total, per annum, - - - - -	$26,400 00

This Company, in consideration of their taking such new lease and paying such increased rent, to have the right, upon the canceling of the bonds, to require the issue to them of stock of the Cambridge Railroad Company for the same amount, provided this Company will agree to pay the semi-annual dividend of 4½ per cent. thereon.

WALTHAM AND WATERTOWN RAILWAY, BOSTON.

This road was leased to the Union Railway Company, April 11, 1857, (which lease was confirmed by the stockholders, July 6, 1857), for the term of ten years, for the sum of fifteen hundred dollars per annum, from May, 1857, payable semi annually on the first days of July and January—with the privilege of renewing the same for five years longer, at the same rate—they to keep the road in good repair at their own expense.

STATEMENT OF THE UNION RAILWAY COMPANY, BOSTON,

For the year ending November 30th, 1858.

Cost of the Road.

The Cambridge Railroad was built by contract for the sum of - -	$300,000 00	
Extra work not included in contract.		
For alterations of road, lengthening switches and turnouts, &c., &c., -	1,075 21	
For lumber and iron work required for alterations, - - - -	1,259 61	
For paving, paving stones and gravel,	2,303 67	
For engineering, - - - -	4,625 00	
For interest, salaries of officers, &c., &c., during construction, - -	7,513 65	
		$316,777 14
Amount carried forward,		$316,777 14

Cost of Equipment.

Amount brought forward,		$316,777 14
35 cars, valued at - - -	$23,950 00	
251 horses, valued at $112 50 each,	28,237 50	
Omnibuses, sleighs, &c., valued at	940 00	
Cost of land and buildings thereon when purchased, - - -	42,636 64	
Cost of buildings, offices, stables, &c., erected by the Company, - -	10,701 02	
Cost of sundry articles, harness, stable furniture, tools, &c., &c., - -	9,267 49	
Lumber on hand, - - -	1,851 41	
Provender on hand, - - -	1,988 95	
Expended toward the construction of new cars, - - - - -	711 86	
In addition to the above sums, the company has charged to the equipment account, at various times since it was organized, for various items connected with its operations, including loss on old omnibuses, horses, &c., construction of new tracks, turn-outs, &c., &c., -	39,703 17	
		159,988 04
Total cost of construction and equipment,		$476,765 18

The exact cost of the various articles of the company's equipment cannot be given. A portion of the cars were purchased and a portion built by the company; the cost of the materials used therefor cannot be separated from the cost of the other articles required for ordinary repairs, and the entire cost of the materials used in building the cars has therefore been included in the Repair

Account. The mechanics employed in building such new cars having also been employed on the ordinary repairs of the equipment, the time cannot be separated, and their entire wages have, therefore, been included in the Wages Account. The same remark applies, also, to snow plows built in the company's work shops, and to a few other articles of the equipment. The horses are always valued upon the company's books at $112 50 each, and whatever loss may be made beyond that sum, either by purchasing new horses at a higher price than that, or by the exchange of old horses for new ones, is ascertained every three months, and the amount then included among the running expenses of the company, —as may be noticed in the statement of running expenses hereafter given in this return. The Real Estate owned by the company is always valued, upon their books, at its original cost; the cost of all new buildings erected thereon, such as car houses, stables, work shops, &c., together with all alterations and repairs, being included in the running expenses under the head of Repairs of Real Estate. The cost of all the other articles of equipment is included among the running expenses, and every six months an inventory of the entire equipment is taken, in which the buildings, cars and other articles are appraised by a Committee of the Board of Directors at their value to the company, the appraised value in no case, however, exceeding the cost. In consequence of the adoption of this plan, there is no necessity for any charge for depreciation, for should any article of equipment be worn out and become of no value during any six months, that article does not appear in the next inventory of the company's property, and the difference between the amount of the last and former inventory will be included among the expenses; on the contrary, if the article worn out has been replaced by another of the same value, the amount of the inventory remains the same and the cost of renewing is included, where it should be, among the running expenses; the cost of the new article having been charged to Expense Account at the time of purchase. But if the amount of the inventory is increased by new articles purchased during the preceding six months, and which have been charged among the expenses, the difference between the last and the former inventory is then credited to the company as a part of their profit.

Total earnings during the year.

From passengers, - - - -	$150,852 28	
From U. S. Mails, - - -	466 66	
From sales of manure, - - -	1,093 01	
From other sources, - - -	2,407 00	
		$154,818 95

Expenses of operating the road.

For repairs of road, buildings, &c.,	$6,407 58	
For interest, taxes and insurance, -	4,843 75	
For general repairs, cars, harness, shoeing, &c., &c., - - -	5,952 05	
For all wages, printing, salaries, office expenses, &c., - - - -	57,804 86	
For provender, - - - -	24,437 28	
Amounts carried forward,	$99,445 52	$154,818 95

Amounts brought forward,	$99,445 52	$154,818 95
For miscellaneous articles, blankets, &c.,	1,108 97	
For all other expenses, - - -	5,451 27	
	$106,005 76	
For rent of road, - - - -	28,775 00	
		134,780 76
Net earnings, - - - - - -		$20,038 19
Surplus earnings of previous year, - -		10,140 35
Total, - - - - - -		$30,178 54

Total per centage of dividends at the rate of 10.58 per cent. per annum, leaving a surplus of $6,178 54.

Average number of horses to each car, 7.

Average cost of maintaining each car per day, including wear and tear, feed, salaries, depreciation of property, repairs of road, &c., $10 50.

Average number of miles run by each car, 12,980 per annum.

Average number of passengers carried by each car, 50,120 per annum.

Average cost of carrying each passenger, $7\frac{5}{8}$ cents.

Average cost of mile run, $29\frac{66}{100}$ cents.

Rate of speed, 8 miles per hour.

The total length of rail on this road is equal to that of a single track $9\frac{1}{2}$ miles in length; the track is paved throughout.

THE METROPOLITAN RAILWAY COMPANY, BOSTON.

For the year ending November 30th, 1858.

Cost of the Road.

Amount expended for labor in excavating for the track, laying foundation and rails,	$23,932 99
Amount carried forward,	$23,932 99

Amount brought forward,	$23,932 99	
Amount expended for timber for foundation, - - - - - -	19,952 79	
Amount expended for iron, chairs, spikes, &c., &c., - - -	90,440 36	
Amount expended for paving, and paving stones, - - - - -	34,367 11	
Amount expended for engineering,	5,485 06	
Amount expended for interest, salaries of officers during construction of road, and other expenses, -	68,963 46	
Total cost of road, - - -	$243,141 77	
Amount included in the present and in the past years, among the running expenses, for estimated or actual depreciation of the road, -	16,500 00	
Net cost of road, - - - - -		$226,641 77

Cost of Equipment.

44 cars, valued at - - -	$37,457 90	
528 horses, valued at - - -	70,705 94	
Cost of omnibuses, sleighs, &c., &c., owned by the company, - -	48,524 00	
Cost of land, and buildings thereon when purchased, less mortgages $55,879 16, - - - -	22,559 09	
Cost of buildings, offices, stables, &c.,	24,148 00	
Cost of snow plows, harness, stable fixtures, tools, &c., &c., - -	18,447 71	
Total cost of equipment, - -	$221,842 64	
Amount included in the present and in past years, in the running expenses, for estimated depreciation,	3,500 00	
		218,342 64
Cost of construction and equipment,		$444,984 41

Total Earnings during the year.

From passengers in cars and omnibuses, - - - - -	$273,544 41	
From U. S. Mails, - - -	125 00	
From sales of manure, - - -	4,220 20	
From other sources, - - -	7,905 95	
Total earnings, - - - -		$285,795 56

Expenses for working the Road.

For repairs of road and buildings, -	$4,925 59	
For repairs of cars, shoeing horses, &c.,	10,254 83	
For wages of every person regularly employed, excepting President, Directors, Superintendent and Treasurer, - - - - -	90,173 59	
For interest, taxes and insurance, -	6,954 78	
For rent paid other companies for use of their road, - - - -	2,690 00	
For provender, - - - -	57,105 82	
For miscellaneous articles, blankets, &c.,	874 01	
For loss on horses—that isto say, the difference between the present estimated value of the horses owned by the company, subtracted from the estimated value of those on hand at the commencement of the year—giving the present estimated value of each horse, $134, - - -	10,110 25	
For incidental expenses—including printing, President's, Directors', Treasurer's and Superintendent's salaries, and all expenses other than those belonging to the actual working of the road, and for all other expenses, - - - - - -	27,963 55	
Amounts carried forward,	$211,052 42	$285,795 56

Amounts brought forward,	$211,052 42	$285,795 56
For amount charged on the company's books during the year, for estimated depreciation of the road, - -	10,000 00	
Total expenses, - - - -		221,052 42
Net earnings, - - - -		64,743 14
Surplus earnings of previous year, on hand,		1,797 63
Total surplus for payment of dividends,		66,540 77
Dividend of eight per cent. declared during the year, - - - - - -		32,152 00
Present surplus, - - - -		34,388 77

Average number of horses to each car, 12.

Gross average cost of maintaining each car per day, including wear and tear, $13 76.

Average number of miles run in one year by each car, 16,965.

Average number of passengers carried in each car in one year, 102,844.

Average cost of carrying each passenger, $4\frac{7}{8}$ cents.

Average cost of mile run, $29\frac{1}{2}$ cents.

Rate of speed, $5\frac{1}{2}$ miles per hour.

The total length of rail on this road is equal to a single track of 12 miles—it is paved throughout.

MALDEN AND MELROSE RAILROAD COMPANY, BOSTON.

For eight months ending November, 1858.

Cost of the road, - - - -		$56,106 38

Cost of equipment.

28 cars, - - - - -	$21,850 14	
225 horses, - - - - -	28,125 00	
Amounts carried forward,	$49,975 14	$56,106 38

Amounts brought forward,	$49,975 14	$56,106 38
Cost of omnibuses, sleighs and other vehicles, - - - - - -	10,173 16	
Cost of land and buildings, - -	16,607 27	
Cost of harness, snow plows, tools, &c.,	11,256 09	
Extensions of Middlesex Road in Charlestown and Boston, and switches and turnouts, and the lease of the Middlesex Railroad for forty-seven years, with privileges purchased by this company, with other things, and estimated altogether, - - - - - -	100,000 00	
Total cost of equipment, - -	$188,011 66	
Amount included in the present and in past years in the running expenses for estimated or actual depreciation of any of the above items,	1,569 73	
		186,441 93
Total cost of construction and equipment,		$242,548 31

Total earnings during the eight months.

From passengers, - - -	$61,741 53	
From sales of manure, - - -	546 87	
From other sources, (rents,) - -	1,086 50	
Total earnings, - - - - -		63,374 90

Expenses for working the road.

For repairs of road and buildings,	$1,338 45	
For repairs of cars, harness, shoeing horses, &c., - - - - -	1,685 35	
For interest, taxes and insurance, -	1,814 41	
Amounts carried forward,	$4,838 21	$63,374 90

Amounts brought forward,	$4,838 21	$63,374 90
For rent paid to Middlesex Railroad Company for use of their road, -	13,292 42	
For wages of persons regularly employed, except President, Directors, &c., &c., - - - - - -	20,506 84	
For provender, - - - -	12,046 03	
For incidental expenses, salaries, printing, &c., &c., - - -	3,803 69	
Estimated depreciation of property,	1,569 73	
Total expenses - - - - -		56,056 92
Net earnings, - - - - -		$7,317 98

Average number of horses to each car, 8.

Average cost of maintaining each car per day, including wear and tear, repairs of road, &c., &c., $8 23.

Number of miles run by each car in 8 months, 4,215.

Number of passengers carried by each car in 8 months, 41,369.

Average cost of carrying each passenger, $4\frac{83}{100}$ cents.

Average cost of mile run, 47 cents.

Rate of speed, 6 miles per hour.

The total length of rail on this road is equal to a single track of 12 miles—it is paved throughout.

MIDDLESEX RAILROAD.

This road is leased to the Malden and Melrose Company, who pay a semi-annual rental equal to eight per cent. per annum on each share of the capital stock of the Middlesex Railroad Company.

BROADWAY (HORSE) RAILROAD COMPANY, BOSTON.

This company has had a location granted to it by the Mayor and Aldermen of the City of Boston, and the railroad is under contract for building. A portion of the same is completed, and in operation. The company has bought no real estate, nor any equipment, and no returns have yet been made.

THE DORCHESTER RAILWAY COMPANY.

This company has purchased the corporate property of the Dorchester Avenue Railroad Company, and leased the road—the lessees have run the cars and the line of coaches connected therewith, on their own account, paying to this Corporation a rent equal to eight per cent. per annum on the amount of stock outstanding.

RECAPITULATION OF THE FOREGOING.

NAME OF ROAD.	Cost of Construction.	Cost of Equipment.	Net Profit.
Sixth Avenue	$555,012 62	$199,944 60	$78,125 39
Brooklyn City	574,003 75	452,706 23	99,189 64
Third Avenue	1,000,000 00	170,000 00	117,882 04
Cambridge and Union	316,777 14	159,988 04	20,038 19
Metropolitan	226,641 77	218,342 64	64,743 14
Malden and Melrose	56,106 38	186,441 93	7,317 98
Totals	$2,728,541 66	$1,387,423 44	$387,296 38

Total stated cost of construction and equipment, $4,115,965 10, which, allowing for wear and tear and every expense, has produced a net profit of $387,296, equal to nearly 9½ per cent. per annum.

The above roads comprise a length of single track equal to ninety miles, the amount for construction of such length, including all materials and work, need not now exceed, where no grading or bridges

are necessary, - - - - -	$1,000,000 00
Add cost of buildings and equipment, -	1,387,423 44
	$2,387,423 44

Which would have given a net revenue of $387,296, or more than 16 per cent.

The difference in these two totals arises partly from cost of buying up the omnibus interests.

These statistics show that the business of street railways is of steadily increasing importance, and that the enterprise has been so far, unquestionably successful. The investments have yielded large and regularly paid dividends, even on amounts of capital charged to construction, which was partly consumed in the purchase of imaginary omnibus rights, and other expenses, amounting in total to nearly treble the actual cost for which roads without grading or bridging can now be built.

CHAPTER III.

The vast amount of capital about to be invested in street railways throughout the great commercial cities of this country, renders every information connected with their history and construction a subject of the deepest interest to municipal authorities, to capitalists, and to the community at large.

In treating on this important subject, great difficulty is experienced on account of the impossibility of conveying adequate information for practical purposes, by means of the press. The want of science and actual practice which has been exhibited in many of these undertakings, and the fruitless attempts at imitation, without a just comprehension of the original nature of the plan, have invariably resulted in injury to the road, a tax on the public, and a derangement of the finances of the company.

Gratuitous services are but temporary, and generally terminate in disappointed expectations. Skill and executive labor must be adequately paid for, if expected to be constantly and usefully exerted, and if so exerted, the price is no consideration when compared with the advantages derived.

The contents of this chapter will be classified under the following heads:

First.—A slight sketch of the history of tramways.

Secondly.—Their location, grade and gauge.

Thirdly.—Drainage.

Lastly.—Their mechanical construction.

The earliest account given of the use of tramways, dates as far back as 1670, when, on the introduction of coal as a substitute for wood fuel, great difficulties were experienced in its transportation from the mines to the ships, which was done in rude carts, over rough roads, involving serious expenditures to the proprietors of the mines, who necessarily employed several hundred horses and carts for this traffic. The importance of adopting some plan of reducing the consequent expense, occupied the attention of those interested, and, after serious consideration, the result was the construction of wooden tramways, consisting of straight pieces of timber imbedded longitudinally in the roadway without cross ties.

These were found to be so advantageous that they were at once adopted throughout the mining districts; their construction, as improved, has been thus described:

Some attention appears to have been given to the locations, as considerable deviations from direct lines were made to avoid inequalities of the ground, and consequent expenditure for graduation; the road-bed being leveled, cross ties of large logs of wood, cut into lengths to correspond with the width of the road, were laid across at short distances, and firmly imbedded, to support the longitudinal pieces of timber which were connected end to end over the cross ties, and to which they were nailed or otherwise secured. These timbers or rails becoming constantly broken or rapidly worn away by the continued friction of the wheels, other smaller pieces of timber were laid over the dilapidated portions, which eventually led to the introduction of a double sleeper throughout the whole line. The roadway was generally about six feet wide, the cross ties were laid two feet apart; the under rail was first laid with oak, but afterwards of pine fir, about six feet long, five inches broad, by four or five inches in depth; the upper rail was of the same dimensions, and generally of beech or plane tree; the under rail being properly secured to the cross ties, the road was ballasted with ashes or other material, packed firmly to the surface of the rail, upon which the upper rail was then placed and firmly secured by wooden pins.

The wagons resembled somewhat the coal cars now in use, the wheels were of wood, and very low. Three tons was the general load to each horse. The passage of the wagons over the steep declivities or "runs," was regulated by rude brakes, the management of which, depending upon the dexterity of the wagoners, often produced very fatal results.

The substitution of iron rails for wood, which enabled the horse to haul double his previous load, was introduced about the year 1767, at the iron works of Colebrook Dale. It is said, that the price of iron becoming very low, and the works of this company being of great extent, the pig iron, instead of being stacked, was laid upon the wooden rails, on the supposition that the saving in repair of the rails would help to pay the interest, until the price of iron should rise, when it could be easily taken up and sent away as pig iron. These pieces of iron were about five feet long, four inches broad, and one inch and a quarter thick, with three holes by which they were fastened to the rails. The introduction of the iron rail so reduced the resistance in descending inclined planes that the brake was ineffectual in counteracting the force of gravity, and recourse was had to other modes of restraining the velocity of the wagons, which resulted in the employment of the surplus gravity of the load descending one plane to drag the empty ones up the ascending plane.

The next improvement was the introduction, about the year 1776, of the cast iron tram plates with an upright ledge; since then the subject has so occupied the ingenuity of mechanics and engineers that a great variety of patterns for iron rails have been patented and introduced; of the more modern and useful ones notice will hereafter be taken.

In the year 1825, the Stockton and Darlington Railway was opened; animal power was principally employed, and the community was surprised at the wonderful superiority of railroads over the best of common roads; as a carriage containing twenty-six persons, with their proportion of baggage, was drawn by a single horse at the rate of six miles per hour, with comparatively little exertion.

LOCATION, GRADE AND GAUGE.

The great improvements which have taken place in road-making; consisting, not only in planking, paving, macadamising, &c., but in the greater attention given to the character of gradients for roads adapted only to ordinary vehicles, afford great facilities for the construction of tramways on the line of public roads. The simple act of laying strips of iron on the line and grade of a turnpike or plank road, is certainly not so extensive an undertaking, although a much greater improvement upon the present paved, planked or macadamized road, than these latter were upon the rude roads of former times: in fact the experience gained from tramways now in use, appears to suggest the substitution of the iron way as the next gradual and natural improvement over the ordinary roads.

There are few public roads (having sufficient business to support a tramway) which have not abundance of width for the construction of a railway on their sides without in the slightest impeding the traveling of carriages, wagons, &c., upon their centres; or which could not be advantageously widened by the substitution of a proper plan of drainage for their wide, shallow and useless ditches and pools of stagnant water.

The desiderata in constructing a street railway are economy of motive power, rapidity, safety and public convenience; and whilst it is important, so to locate and construct a railway as to conform to these requirements; economy dictates, that having made a safe calculation of the probable amount of receipts and working expenses, the cost of construction should in all cases be proportioned thereto; but great care should be exercised, for prospective profit, which by figures is capable of easy demonstration, is too often in practice, productive of opposite results.

If, by an extraordinary expenditure, a railway could be so perfectly constructed, that no repairs would be requisite, and that a vastly increased amount of passengers could be transported with the least power; it may be questionable if true economy, owing to the particular circumstances of the company's affairs, might not dictate the construction of a cheaper work, on which a smaller load could be drawn with the same power.

In the location of a passenger tramway on the suburbs of a city, the nature of its business usually confines the route to the public roads, in the immediate vicinity of which, those who constitute its permanent travel reside. No deviation therefrom can consequently be admissible, and as to the question whether to grade, or to lay the rail on the existing surface of the road; it is a matter to be determined by the cost; by questions arising out of local circumstances; or in some cases, by the general railroad law of the State.

It is conceded that the level road is less fatiguing to horses, than that which is undulating; and therefore it is desirable in constructing a tramway, to lay the superstructure on such grades, as will allow the horses to ascend without too much exertion and descend without risk or danger on a road covered with ice and snow.

In order to determine what shall be the maximum gradient; it is necessary to consider the question alternately, as an ascent and descent—the former concerns the economy of motive power; the latter, the safety of rapid traveling.

There are many circumstances which affect the motion of cars on a street railway, and in investigating the subject as to what may be the maximum of ascending grade, where horse-power is employed, the following will be noticed as the most important points to be considered:

The maximum load.

Traction due the maximum load on a level.

Available power—from which must be deduced the maximum gradients to be adopted in location—thus:

The two-horse car in ordinary use, weighs	4,200 lbs.
Capable of carrying 30 passengers, whose average weight will not exceed 150 lbs.,	4,500 "
Maximum load, - - - - -	8,700 lbs.

On a level the tractive force is expended merely to overcome friction; which on iron railways is calculated from $\frac{1}{150}$ to $\frac{1}{200}$ of the load, according to the dryness or dampness of the rails; but on street railways may more correctly be estimated at $\frac{1}{120}$ of the load, on account of the extraneous matter liable to accumulate on the rails. Thus then 8,700 lbs. being the maximum load $\frac{120}{8700}$ = 73 lbs. is the traction due the maximum load on a level. The proportion of traction, to load, on gradients is, as the ratio of inclination is to its length—taking the available power of two horses at 327 lbs. we have $\frac{327}{8700}$ = 26, thus the gradient should not exceed 1 in 26.

The resistance here calculated at $\frac{1}{120}$ of the load will vary according to the nature and condition of the road, occasioned by matter on the rails, undulations in the same, whether from imperfection in the iron or want of uniformity in the grades, or unevenness at the joints; all of which have the same injurious effects, as rising over an obstruction, and form a much greater part of the resistance on an iron road, where they are proportionably more injurious than on a turnpike road; and the power of a horse to overcome the same is greatly diminished in proportion to the ascent.

The resistance due wheel carriages is the effect of two separate causes, arising from the attrition on their axes, and the action of the wheel upon the rail. The pressure on the rubbing parts at the axis of a carriage is proportional to the weight of the body of the carriage, and its load. The pressure on the rails will exceed that on the axis by the weight of the wheels, and thus the wheel is prevented sliding on the rail. The resistance decreases in the ratio of the radius of the wheel to the radius of the axle: therefore in the construction of railway cars it is desirable to have the diameter of the wheels as large, and the axles as small, as convenience and safety will allow. The amount of friction to be overcome will vary according to the character of the lubricating material made use of, and the smoothness and evenness of their surfaces; by the uniform cleanness of the rail surface; and the accuracy of the wheel's periphery.

It is next necessary to consider the nature and effect of the power employed to move the cars, and whilst it would be superfluous to add any description of the horse, it is desirable to make such investigation as to its muscular force and power of duration, as will aid its application in such a manner, as to afford the greatest amount of useful effect, with as much speed as can be obtained without injury to the animal.

In conducting the business of conveying passengers on street railways, speed is secondary only to safety; and the daily work of a horse thus employed is to be calculated by distance run, the duration of labor being shortened in proportion to speed.

Dr. Desaguliers estimates the power of a horse at 200 lbs., moving 2½ miles an hour, for 8 hours in a day, making 200 lbs. 20 miles in a day.

Mr. Watt estimates it at 150 lbs., at the same rate.

Mr. Tredgold places it at 125 lbs., at the rate of 3 miles per hour, for 6 hours of a day.

Experiments were made by Mr. Wood, with a very complete model, from which it appears that the tractive force required to move a car on a level railway is capable of being reduced to one-five-hundredth part of the weight; if then the average draught of a horse through a day's work is estimated at 150 lbs., moving at the rate of 2½ miles an hour, the same horse should be capable of hauling on a level railway $500 \times 150 = 75{,}000$ lbs., or about 33½ tons. No railway, however, is so perfectly constructed as to admit of this application.

A horse working every day, traveling 20 miles a day, exerts a force varying from 50 to 300 lbs., the greatest muscular power exerted by average dray horses on steep ascents through the streets, will probably sometimes amount to 400 lbs.

On the colliery railways in England, in one ascent of 236 feet to the mile, one horse hauls 2 tons of coal, and in another, on a plane of 500 feet in length, it is estimated that the muscular force employed by a horse is about 342 lbs.

It is calculated that, taking the load which a horse can draw on a level at 1,

On a rise of	120	feet to the mile,	he can draw only	.75
"	220	"	"	.50
"	528	"	"	.25

The following table by Mr. Tredgold, represents the duration of labor and maximum velocity of a horse unloaded:

Duration of labor,	1 hour.	2 h.	3 h.	4 h.	5 h.	6 h.	7 h.	8 h.	10 h.
Maximum velocity unloaded, in miles per hour,	14.7 miles.	10.4 m.	8.5 m.	7.3 m.	6.6 m.	6 m.	5.5 m.	5.2 m.	4.6 m.

This he considers may be taken as very nearly the law of decrease of speed by increased duration of labor when a horse moves on a level road, unloaded. If the road be inclined, the velocity of ascent will decrease in proportion to the rise of the inclination, and proportionally increase in the descent.

From calculation it would appear that a horse can haul seven times a greater weight on a level road than he can on an inclination of 5 in 100, and practical experience proves that on a line of five miles where there are continually undulating grades, varying from level to 5 in 100, two horses can regularly haul four tons in one hour. This then would tend to clearly demonstrate that the system now adopted on level streets of attaching two horses to a car, whose weight when loaded will perhaps not exceed four tons, the capacity of the horses being twenty-eight tons, is a waste of motive power, arising either from a miscalculation of the horses' power, inferiority of stock, or defectiveness in the wheels or track.

Viewing the subject of grades as a descent, there are these dangers, that the brakes may not be properly constructed and attached, and that carelessness in their application may result in serious accidents, and must always cause a greater strain upon the horses in resisting the tendency of the car to roll down the hill. A much more secure plan than the present brake may be adopted on cars running on steep descents, by attaching the moving power of a lever to the tongue or pole of the car, the fulcrum on a plane with the height of the wheel, and using the other arm against the resisting wheel; the brake would then be self-acting, and in the event of the horses falling, the progress of the car would be immediately arrested—moreover, when the road is covered with ice, the slippery surface renders both the ascent and descent troublesome, dangerous to the horses, and sometimes impracticable.

Thus in laying out a railway where the motive power of horses is to be employed, observing the danger and inconvenience of descending inclinations and the increasing loss of power on ascents, it follows that it is highly important to obviate as much as possible all heavy gradients, particularly in the middle portions of a road where the travel will in all probability be heaviest; for the expense of motive power on a level will increase in much greater ratio than the increased rate of inclination.

Until very recently, the shortest radius of curvature adopted on main lines was sixty feet, and of the pattern shown in plate 14, the difficulty experienced in turning some of the sharp angles of the streets was, in one case, so great as to interfere with a proper location of the track, and much inventive genius was applied (as is not unfrequently the case) to remedy the evil without consideration of its cause; thus every conceivable alteration to the car was suggested. The matter was referred to Strickland Kneass, Esq., the Chief Engineer and Surveyor of the city of Philadelphia, who, upon investigation, decided to remedy the evil in the pattern of the rail. By placing a car on the curve it was observed that the distance between the wheels was so great as to cause the flange of the back wheel to "ride" on the oblique line of the rail edge to the surface of rail and pass over it—the pattern of rail was altered to that shown in plate 13, where the wagon edge of rail rising at right angles, prevents the flange of the wheel having any purchase thereon other than that afforded by the inclination of flange, which is counteracted by the weight of the car.

DRAINAGE.

The drainage of railways demands the most careful consideration, and the judgment of the engineer is required to render available the natural facilities of the country. Not only must the surface water be got rid of, but the adjacent substratum should be thoroughly drained, and protection made from the flood of water in heavy rains. Where springs rise on the site of the road, drains should be made into them; all drains must communicate with the natural water courses of the country, and in some cases it may be necessary to build cross drains of good masonry under the road bed, particularly where it is located on the slope of a hill. Where no provision is made for drainage, not only will the timbers soon decay, but the soil which forms the bed or foundation of the structure, becoming loose, recedes from the timbers, and the effect of every additional weight on the rail, causes a deflection and consequent vibration at the joints, abrupt changes in the grade and increased wear and tear in the material of which the road is constructed. It is not difficult to perceive that the subject of drainage is one of the first importance in the construction of tramways, and that even with enormous expenditures, it is useless to attempt to keep a suburban railway in repair, under an incomplete system of drainage. The side channels and all the road drains require a thorough examination at the commencement of spring and winter, and *constant attention* to their being kept free from obstruction; by this means the road will be kept dry and be maintained in good condition at proportionally small expense.

The gauge of track and pattern of rail to be adopted are questions of the greatest importance, on the judicious decision of which will depend in a great measure the local popularity of street railways. Philadelphia, though slow to introduce a new system of locomotion to her streets, has so consulted the requirements of the public generally by improving on the plans of other cities, as to accommodate those who use the streets with private vehicles, as well as those who travel in the cars.

Under an ordinance of City Councils of Philadelphia, all iron rails laid in the streets must be of the pattern shown in plate 12, and the gauge of track five feet two inches, the space between the wheels of ordinary vehicles. Under this arrangement the broad tramway of the rail provides a smooth iron surface for the wheels of carriages, wagons, drays, &c., and accomplishes the advantages of concentrating the travel, relieving the streets of the noise occasioned by the rattling of heavily laden vehicles over the rough stones, economizing a heavy annual expense for repairing streets; and by accommodating all classes of the community, the prejudice and opposition which formerly existed are gradually being forgotten.

The engineering of some of the first railways laid down in Philadelphia was entrusted to the eminent Chief Engineer and Surveyor of the city, and, how thoroughly he appreciated the requirements and interests of the city, as well as the convenience of the public, is evident, from the manner in which practical experience has substantiated his opinions herein expressed.

"*Philadelphia, October* 12*th*, 1855.

J. M. GIBSON, ESQ.,

Chairman of Special Committee on City Passenger Railroads,

DEAR SIR:—Having conferred with your committee regarding the subject of City Passenger Railroads, and in company with you visited lines for proposed routes, I beg leave to offer a few remarks preparatory to your report to Councils, that will bear more especially upon their usefulness and mode of construction than upon the policy to be adopted for their general management, which, strictly, is the province of your body.

As to their general usefulness, we can take as a precedent upon which to base an opinion, the great advantage that the present omnibus system, imperfect as it is, affords to all classes of our community. The rapid increase in the number of omnibus lines, each yielding a handsome revenue upon the investment, proves conclusively the large number benefited; and the saving of time to those whose residences are at a distance from the business mart, as well as the benefits accruing to the merchant in rendering his store or counting-house accessible from all sections of the city without fatigue or loss of valuable time, will secure the hearty co-operation to any improvements in the present arrangements that may be suggested.

The advantage of a railroad car over an omnibus, as now used, is self-evident, not only to the passengers, but to those who may reside upon the streets through which the route may be located. The construction of the cars is such as to afford the greatest comfort to passengers, not only in their ingress and egress, but while passing to their destination—the width of the car being equal to the distance from hub to hub of an ordinary coach. The interior proportions will be sufficiently large to avoid many discomforts now so justly complained of.

To the residents upon the route one great advantage will be the relief from the incessant din attendant upon the rapid transit of heavy coaches, so injurious to the invalid, and now urged by many as a serious objection to living upon an omnibus route; their rapidity of motion and security will also be at once appreciated—moving, as they can, more rapidly, with less noise and greater safety than the cumbrous vehicles that now, to accommodate a passenger, or to avoid apparent danger, depend upon the strength of the driver and the willingness of stubborn horses; while with a city passenger *car*, the horses require no lines, further than for guidance around curves and keeping them within the track; the application of a well arranged brake alone causing, if necessary, an instantaneous stoppage. They are, therefore, in crowded thoroughfares attended with much less danger than vehicles of ordinary construction and similar motive power.

Their introduction will prevent the streets being, as now, blocked by a double, and frequently a treble row of coaches, creating an intolerable annoyance to the business man, and will afford to the community greater accommodations in every particular wherein they consider the present system advantageous.

The rail that I should recommend for the use of a city track, as arriving at more nearly the requirements than any other in use, is similar, though differing somewhat in detail, to the iron now laid at the intersection of Third and Chestnut streets designed and placed there some years since, at the instigation of our enterprising fellow citizen, Jesse Godley, Esq. The constant use to which it has been subjected without derangement, placed at the intersection of two of the greatest thoroughfares within the limits of our city, proves its value.

In differing from that rail I should form one unsuited for locomotive engine and train, by reducing the height and increasing the inclination of the wagon-edge, thereby allowing ordinary vehicles to cross and recross, as well as diverge from its line without fear of injury, at the same time offering sufficient obstruction to the flange of the car-wheel, to prevent an escape from the track, unless by an obstacle purposely placed there.

The formation of the track should be of the usual plan of cross-tie and longitudinal stringer, laid in ballast of broken stone or coarsely sifted gravel; the first, unless the gravel be very coarse and entirely free from loam, being preferable as affording stability, at the same time offering free opportunity for the percolation of water that would otherwise remain around and injuriously affect the imbedded timber.

The rail-fastening I prefer to be made, notwithstanding many objections have been offered, with a clinch spike and counter sunk head, driven through the bed of the rail; experience shows that they hold the rail more firmly than side spiking, which has but comparatively small hold of the stringer, while the objection made, that surface spiking permits water to penetrate the timber, applies in both plans.

The gauge to be adopted is a question worthy of much consideration, and I should recommend that it be made to conform to that of the ordinary carriages in use upon our highways, notwithstanding a combined rail would be necessary in the event of Third street being selected for a city route.

As these roads will be located and constructed for specific purposes and not adapted for the cars of freight roads, there is no reason why the old gauge of four feet eight and a half inches should be retained, while a great reduction in the expense of maintenance of way will be the result of a change. The old gauge is such as to allow vehicles the use of only one wheel upon the rail, while the other travels upon a line formed by the iron and paving, the constant use of which soon creates a rut requiring constant attention and expense to keep in repair. This is the case even with cubical blocks, as evidenced on the line of Third street.

For the formation of a perfect track, cubical block paving at the side of the rail is imperative and when the street is formed with cobble stones, the blocks should be laid alternate, long and short, so as to destroy as much as possible *the line,* which would be the nucleus of a rut.

By increasing the gauge to five feet two inches, vehicles traveling upon the track, will use both rails without injury to the iron or pavement, and the wagon-edge of the rail will offer no impediment to turning out, should a heavy team be overtaken by a car, and will cause an increased revenue to draymen, carters, &c., by enabling them to haul a larger amount more expeditiously with the same horses.

The mere circumstance of having a railroad track properly constructed upon a street, which to many seems an insuperable objection, is, in my opinion, none whatever, when that track is used solely by horse power.

One great difficulty regarding its introduction, is to dispel from the minds of those who are most strenuous in their opposition, the idea of an extended train of heavily laden cars, drawn at a great and unmanageable velocity by steam power, or where this extreme is not reached, we have the effect of the imperfect track on Third street to combat; but, the roads under consideration are for the use of the same motive power as the carriages for which is claimed the exclusive right of the highways, and offers less obstruction and danger than an omnibus whose course is erratic, frequently producing a fractured axle or wheel when least expected.

The objection to a single track in the middle of a fifty feet street, as interfering with the requirements of adjoining tenements is one which will be waived so soon as the experiment is made, for in all cases the carriage-way is twenty-six feet wide, giving a clear space on each side of the rails of ten feet five inches, and of the car in passing—which is but momentary—nine feet six inches, sufficient for all household purposes, and offers no impediment to builders when occupying the street with materials of construction, as it infringes but six inches upon the distance from curb, now allowed them by law.

The further objection, that the passage of cars will interfere with the traffic upon the highways is equally untenable, as they will, in fact, be advantageous in keeping the current more perfect; for, should a street be occupied to its legal limits with building materials, there is but room for the passage of *two vehicles;* they are therefore confined to specified tracks when there are no rails, then why not allow one stream of carriages to take the rails and follow or precede the car—collisions would be less frequent and the constant jams caused by three coaches endeavoring to pass through a space sufficiently wide for two only, would be prevented.

The only objection that has tenure is, that furniture cars and drays will infringe upon the line of rails when backed to the curb. This is by no means serious, for it is never necessary for them to remain in that position so long a time as to seriously delay the car, if compelled to wait even until the load be completed or delivered.

With reference to the location of remunerative routes, I will omit remark, further than that the business men of Councils are more capable of making a judicious selection than any others—the experience of a civil engineer therein being necessary only so far as their applicability to grades suitable for the economical working of the road machinery.

I should at the same time express a hope that an east and west line may receive from you its due consideration as equally useful for the north and west as the other is for the north and south.

As regards the policy that should govern the construction of City Passenger Railroads, I am inclined to the opinion that to secure the true interests of the city, as well as their proper management, they should be built and maintained by the corporation—the city issuing a license for each car to companies who may have each the exclusive use of a certain route, the company to pay annually, an amount that shall be an assessment upon each passenger carried, the rates to be regulated annually from sworn returns made by the officers of the company.

The cars will then bear the same relation to the city that the omnibuses now do, and will prevent incessant clashing between companies that would otherwise be compelled to use a portion of each others' routes; it will place in the power of the city the means to correct abuses, preventing imposition upon its citizens and the creating what should be a public benefit, a nuisance. The city will then know where to look for the proper repair of its highways, and not be, in a measure, dependent upon a company of individuals whose only interest will be the amount of dividends realized.

If it is advisable (and I agree such is the case) that a commencement be made at once, such contracts should be entered into with capitalists who seek the investment, as will enable the city to obtain the possession of the roads as soon as the financial condition of its treasury will permit, or whatever arrangement to reach that point Councils may decide upon.

Very respectfully,

STRICKLAND KNEASS,

Chief Engineer and Surveyor.

This plan was adopted, and has now been in successful operation more than one year. The only objections which have been raised against it are that the flange of the rail, forming an elevation of about $\frac{7}{8}$ of an inch, retains water, dirt, ice, &c., in the trackway, and the trampling of the horses tends to throw stones and dirt outward, which becoming accumulated on the rails, entail a heavy expense to keep the track clean.

It has been suggested that the rails shall be reversed, by which the higher level or flange of rail will be on the inside; the space between the rails may then be sufficiently elevated above the rest of the street to allow the surface water to flow freely away; and that if the lower level or tramway of the rail be manufactured an inch wider, it will be more convenient for vehicles, enabling them to cross the street or turn out of the track with less resistance than is now experienced.

The adoption of this plan will render it necessary to reverse the car wheels, by which the flanges will be on the outside. The objection which first suggests itself to this alteration is, that as the rails have a tendency to spread, a consequent increased friction will be produced by the action of the flange of the wheel on that of the rail.

On a perfect railroad, with perfect machinery, the slightly conical form given to the periphery of the wheels should be sufficient to preserve their parallelism. The flanges are intended to act as guides in running on curves, and guards in cases of accidents. The causes which would produce a friction of the flange of the wheel on the side of the rail are generally a difference in diameter of either of the wheels, obstructions on the rail, a depression of one rail, undulations in the track, and a variety of others, which arise in most cases from neglect. Unless these causes are removed, the track must necessarily spread. Another cause of spreading is the trampling of the horses between the rails, compressing the material, and producing a similar effect to that caused by driving a wedge; this is easily counteracted by ordinary mechanical appliances.

It is not a little surprising that in London and Paris, where so many street improvements have been and are being continually introduced, and where sanitary reform prevails, and every other municipal regulation of street discipline is so strictly enforced, that the old system of street locomotion should still be adhered to; that where spacious thoroughfares are being laid out, and magnificent structures erected, their occupants should be still subjected to the numerous inconveniences so effectually obviated by the city railway.

The improvements recently introduced in the construction of the railway overcome all the obstacles which formerly existed, and there is not an argument that can be urged against the system which cannot be satisfactorily combated by any one conversant with its practical operation. The increase of business caused by increased facilities for traveling, increases the number of employees required; and the magnificent scale upon which these establishments may be conducted in Paris would provide employment for thousands of officials, clerks, conductors, mechanics, drivers, overseers, stable-men, &c., and produce to the government a revenue which will appear surprising and incredible.

MECHANICAL CONSTRUCTION.

In the prosecution of no new work is activity, dispatch, and system in the distribution of material more necessary than in that of a street railway, where the obstruction to travel, the temporary inconvenience to residents on the line of the torn-up street, and consequent danger of infringing upon municipal ordinances are to be constantly held in view. In laying a railway track through a public street there are many matters of detail that require particular attention, such as the crossing of, or junction with other tracks, the crossing of drains or gutters, and other minor difficulties, which in many instances require the exercise of some ingenuity even on the part of a *practical* engineer.

The description of material to be used in the construction of a street railway, will in some measure be determined by local circumstances.

A great variety of timber has been used for cross ties, viz: white oak, chestnut, yellow pine and white pine, &c., hewn or sawed, 5 × 6, and varying in length according to the width of the track, extending at least 12 inches on both sides of the track—the distance between the cross ties varies, as in some instances they are laid six feet apart, in others four feet, and if no stringer be used, about two feet apart: they should be imbedded in trenches cut to receive them, and the earth firmly packed and rammed around them, care being always taken that they rest square and solid and present even and parallel surfaces with the line of grade.

The string pieces or longitudinal timbers, which are used both to elevate and provide a uniform bearing for the rail, may be of Georgia or Carolina yellow pine, or where the quality of this descrtption of timber is inferior, or the price excessive, white pine may be substituted; it is usually cut in lengths varying from twenty to forty feet, and of the dimensions required; that commonly laid down in streets has been seven inches, by the width of the rail; the object in the height of seven inches is, so to elevate the rail as to provide sufficient depth to prevent the horses' feet coming in contact with and destroying the cross ties; the required depth will vary according to the material with which the surface of the road is covered, but in a pitched or paved roadway seven inches is not too much, as allowing sufficient depth for paving over the ties: the width should be the full width of the rail, and its surface planed and grooved to fit the bottom shape of rail; the joints should be made by a scarfing of about four inches in length, reversed on each half, and great care always taken that each joint has an equal and solid bearing on the square face of the cross tie.

Various means have been employed for fastening the stringer to the cross tie; it has been suggested to notch the tie so as to allow the stringer to set in it, but this would result in early decay. Square oak pins, iron bolts and spikes have been used, and much difference of opinion exists as to which is most effective; oak pins are cheapest, and they have this advantage, that they present no obstacle to spiking the iron, if in that operation a spike hole happens over a pin; but there is the danger of their being broken in driving, in which case they may be adzed off and the cross tie allowed to remain unfastened to the stringer. A half inch round wrought iron bolt, with a spike point and slightly battered head, makes a fastening sufficiently secure for the purpose required. The annexed cut, plate 21, represents the spike, bolt and pin which have been separately used for this purpose: the circle at the end of the pin represents the size of the hole which is bored after the ties are set, and into which the pin is driven through stringer and cross tie; the sides of the pin are hollowed out in order to form a draft. Care should always be taken in removing earth or digging trenches for the stringers, not to disturb the soil below the level of the surface of the ties, as it is more solid in its natural state and affords a better bearing, than can be obtained by any process of ramming; but if the soil is of such a nature as will not admit of this uniformity, proper attention should be given to provide for the stringer an even and uniform bearing with the surface of the cross tie. The stringers should be so laid that the joint on one side will be about opposite the middle of the piece on the other side.

Cast-iron knees, or angle-chairs, are sometimes necessary to prevent the track from spreading. These vary in weight from two to ten pounds. They are spiked on each side of the track to the stringer, and to every tie, or alternate tie as may be deemed expedient. The first spike should be always driven into the stringer,—thus the danger of separating it from the cross-tie will be lessened.

The chief item in the cost of material is the iron; and it will be seen by reference to the accompanying drawings, how many patterns have been in use during the short time that street railways have been established. Cast-iron rails have been used; but these are being taken up on account of their inefficiency, and rolled iron substituted.

The Cambridge Railroad, Boston, was originally built with rolled iron, weighing 64 lbs. per yard, of the most approved pattern on any of the New York street roads, and was selected, from the many in use there, by the Mayor and Aldermen of Boston and Cambridge, and by them ordered by vote to be used on this road. No cast iron rails had, up to that time, been used on any street road in New York. They have since been used by this company, as a matter of experiment merely, on their short curves—on the draw of the West Boston Bridge, and for a turnout on the North Avenue Branch—but with the exception of those used on the curves, the cast rails have not worked as satisfactorily as could be desired, and will not be used hereafter.

The form of rail which has given the most general satisfaction is that in use in Philadelphia, which is five inches wide; and, if the width of the tramway were increased one inch, it would be found to afford increased facilities for ordinary vehicles. The iron should be of the best quality of iron manufactured for railroad purposes, perfectly straight, and free from warp or twist, and of a uniform thickness throughout. The bars should be in lengths of twenty-four feet, and cut square at the ends; they should be punched with countersunk holes, in the centre of the rail, at intervals of two feet, and at about two inches from their ends.

The joints of all the rails should rest on a plate of boiler iron, quarter of an inch thick, imbedded in the stringers, and punched with two holes to correspond with the spike-holes at the ends of the rails—care being always taken that the joint of the iron does not happen over the joint of the stringer.

The rails should be spiked at every hole of intervals of two feet; the head of the spike corresponding to the countersink in the rail,—a wrought-iron, flat-headed, clinch spike, six inches long, weighing six ounces, with a larger spike at the joints, will be found sufficient to hold the iron steady.

In crossing the joints of intersecting tracks much inconvenience has been experienced by the jar and consequent wear and tear of cars; this difficulty has been entirely obviated by the improved "frog," see plate 20, for which a patent has been issued. The idea being, to carry the car across the opening of about two inches by allowing the flange of the wheel to run upon the chilled surface in throat of "frog" without affecting the surface of rail.

In surfacing, let great care be observed that an even bearing be always rammed under any tie which may have been raised, or this portion of the track will again be depressed so soon as a load is placed upon the rail.

The material with which the road-bed between the tracks will be filled up, will depend, of course, upon local circumstances. Plank, gravel, block, wood, brick, cast iron, concrete, paving stones, and many other may be used, but it should always be borne in mind that the desideratum is to construct such a surface as will be sufficiently rough to give the horses a secure foothold, but not so much so as to injure their feet,—and herein the interests of the railway company and the public are identical. In filling up the horse-way all sods and vegetable matter should be carefully excluded, and large stones should be broken; the earth should be well packed as it is thrown in, and the surface so formed as to be impermeable, and act as a roof to the portion which it covers. In filling up a track on a paved street, it is desirable to lay for nine or twelve inches on the outside of each rail, large flat paving-stones, to prevent the track spreading.

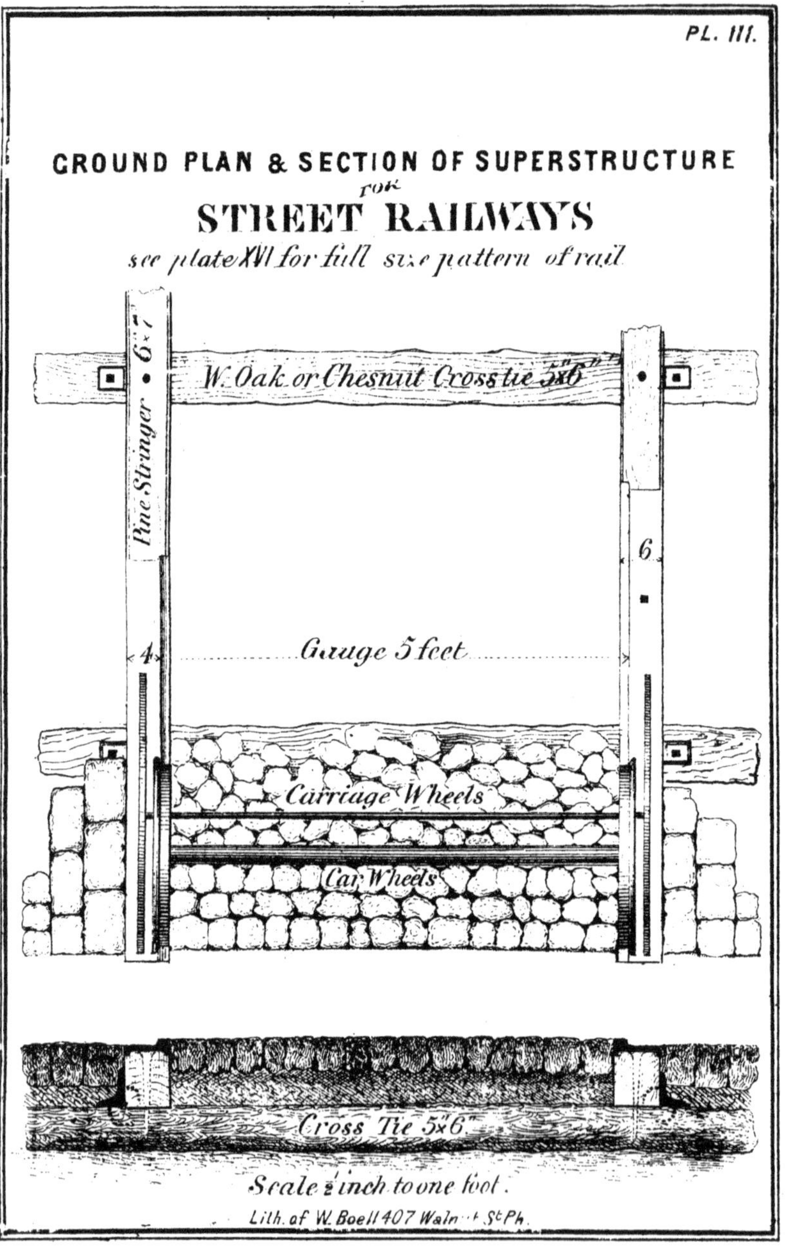
PL. III.
GROUND PLAN & SECTION OF SUPERSTRUCTURE
FOR
STREET RAILWAYS
see plate XVI for full size pattern of rail
Pine Stringer • 6"×7"
W. Oak or Chesnut Cross tie 5"×6"
6
4
Gauge 5 feet
Carriage Wheels
Car Wheels
Cross Tie 5"×6"
Scale ½ inch to one foot.
Lith. of W. Boell 407 Waln^t St Ph.

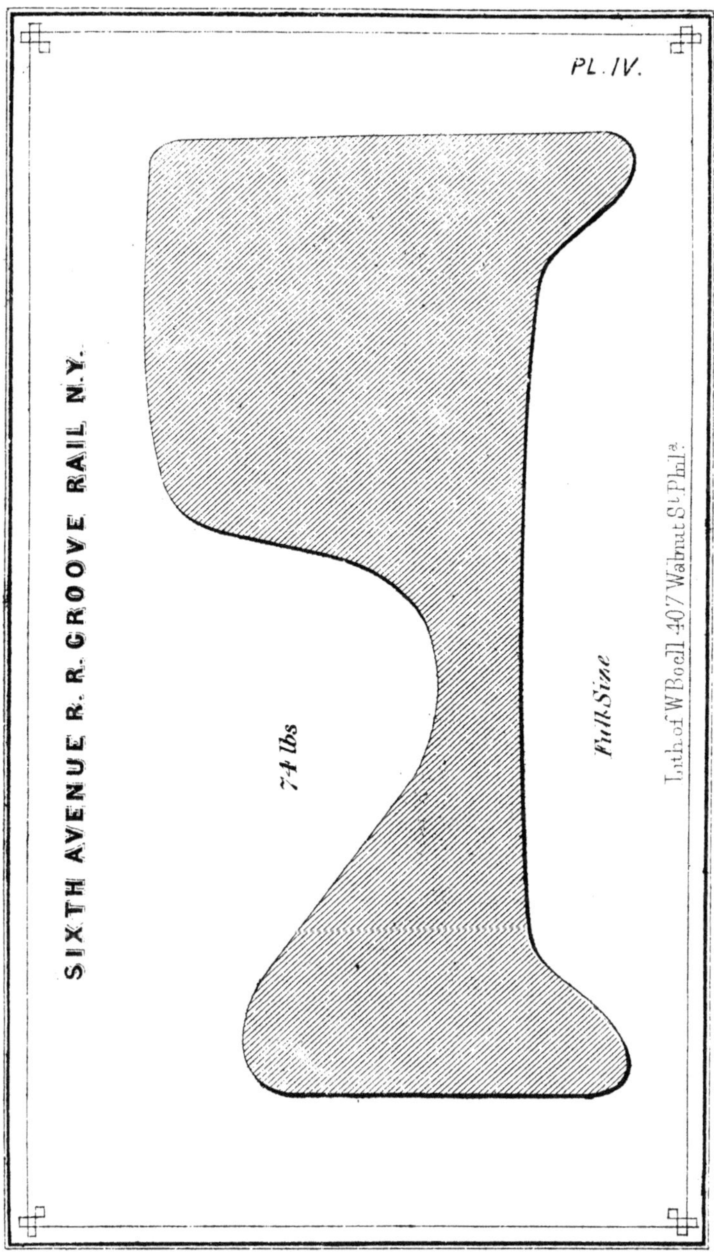
PL. IV.
SIXTH AVENUE R. R. GROOVE RAIL N.Y.
74 lbs
Full Size
Lith. of W Boell 407 Walnut St. Phila

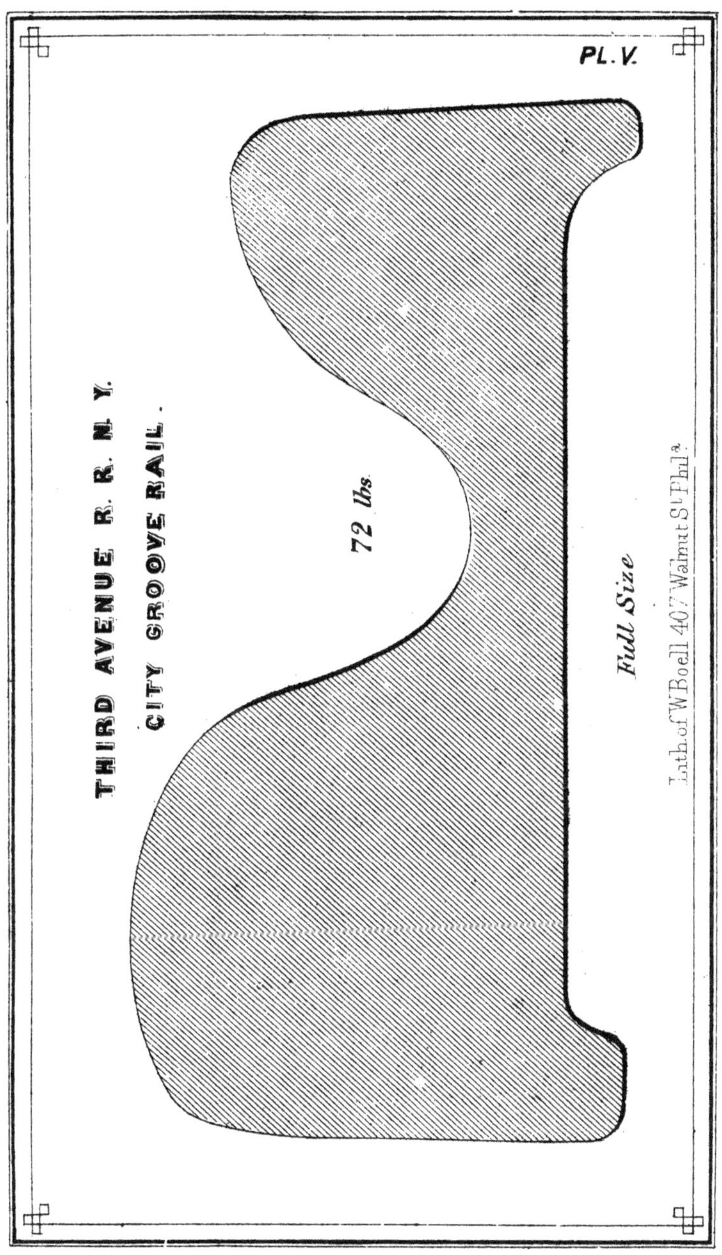
PL. V.
THIRD AVENUE R. R. N. Y.
CITY GROOVE RAIL.
72 lbs.
Full Size
Lith. of W. Boell 407 Walnut St. Phila.

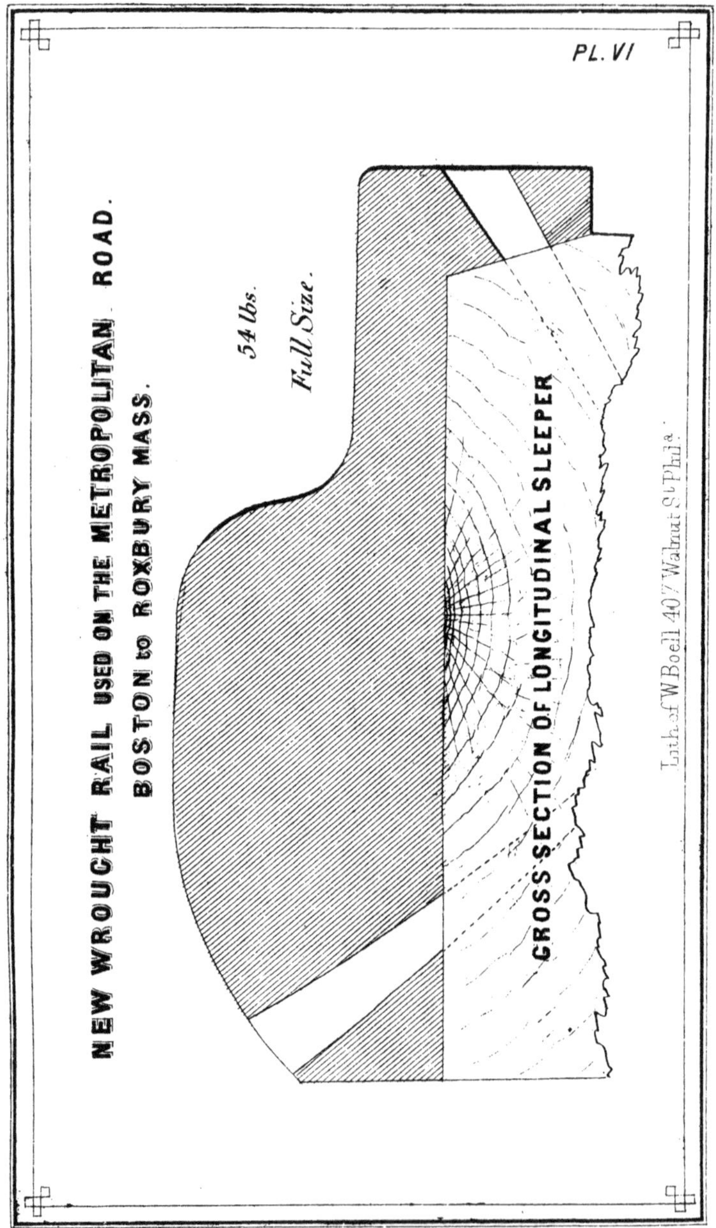
PL. VI
NEW WROUGHT RAIL USED ON THE METROPOLITAN ROAD.
BOSTON to ROXBURY MASS.
54 lbs.
Full Size.
CROSS SECTION OF LONGITUDINAL SLEEPER
Lith. of W. Boell 407 Walnut St. Phila.

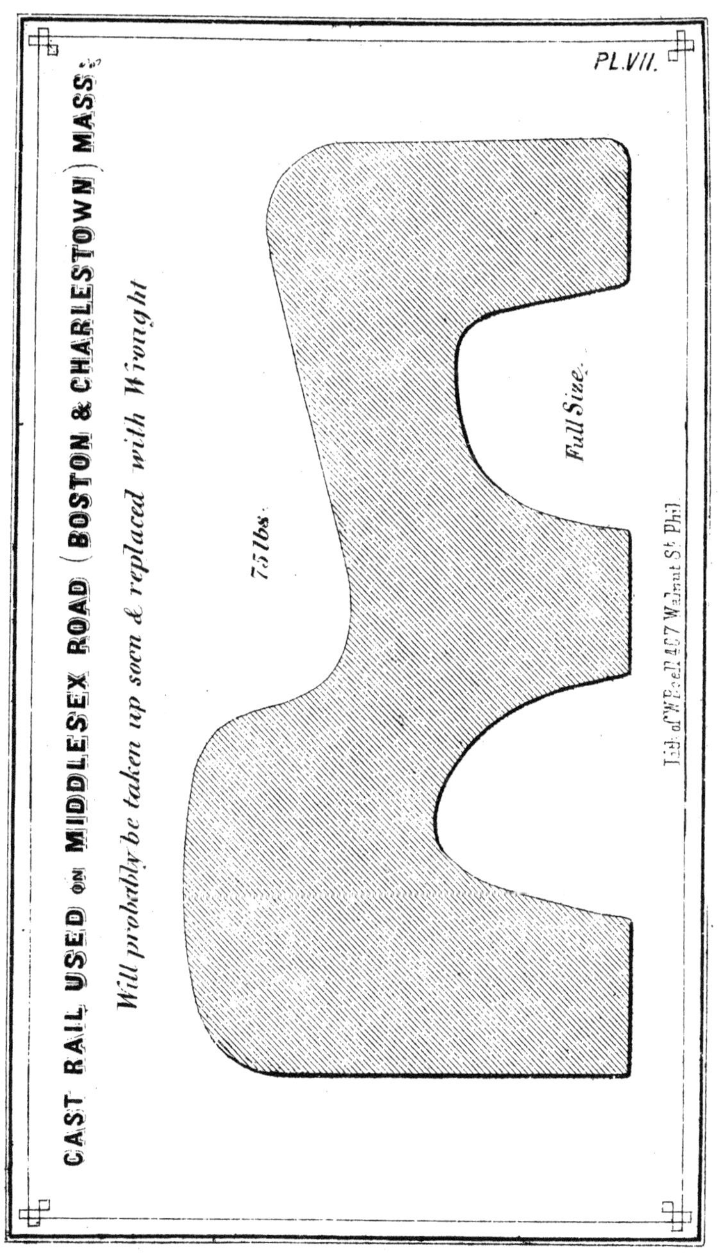
PL.VII.
CAST RAIL USED ON MIDDLESEX ROAD (BOSTON & CHARLESTOWN) MASS.
Will probably be taken up soon & replaced with Wrought
75 lbs.
Full Size.

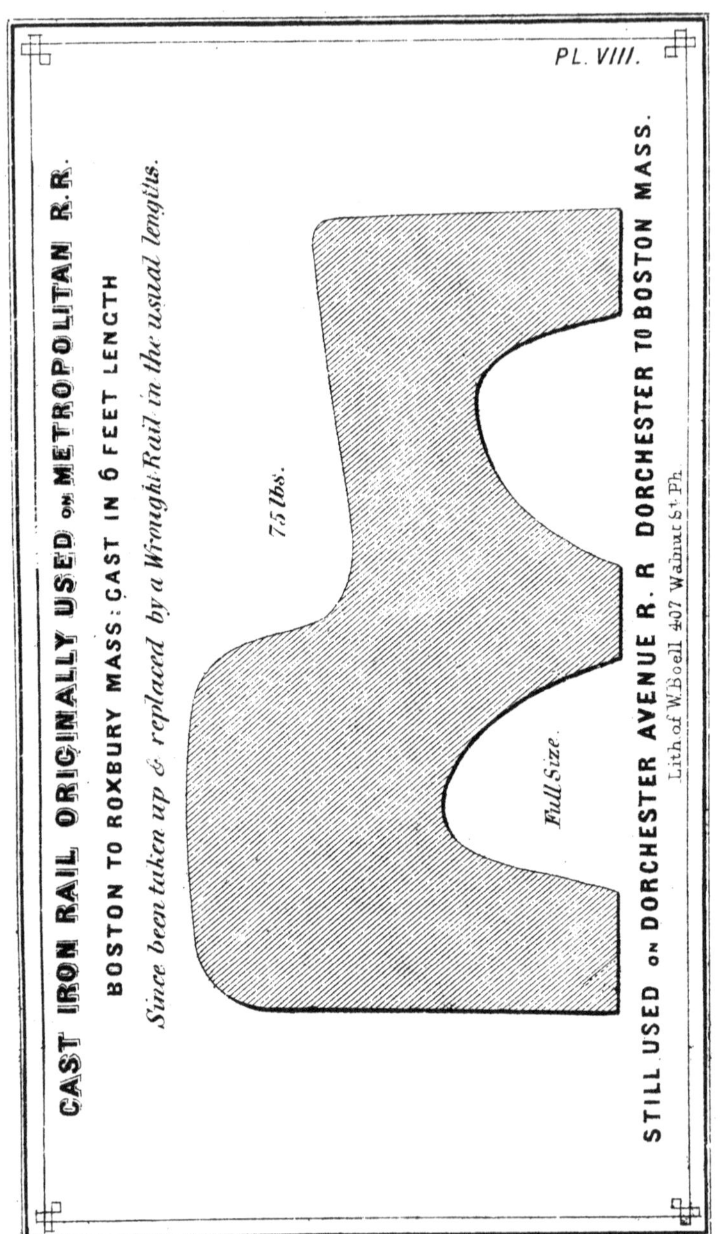
PL. VIII.
CAST IRON RAIL ORIGINALLY USED ON METROPOLITAN R. R.
BOSTON TO ROXBURY MASS: CAST IN 6 FEET LENGTH
Since been taken up & replaced by a Wrought Rail in the usual lengths.
75 lbs.
Full Size.
STILL USED ON DORCHESTER AVENUE R. R. DORCHESTER TO BOSTON MASS.
Lith. of W. Boell 407 Walnut St. Ph.

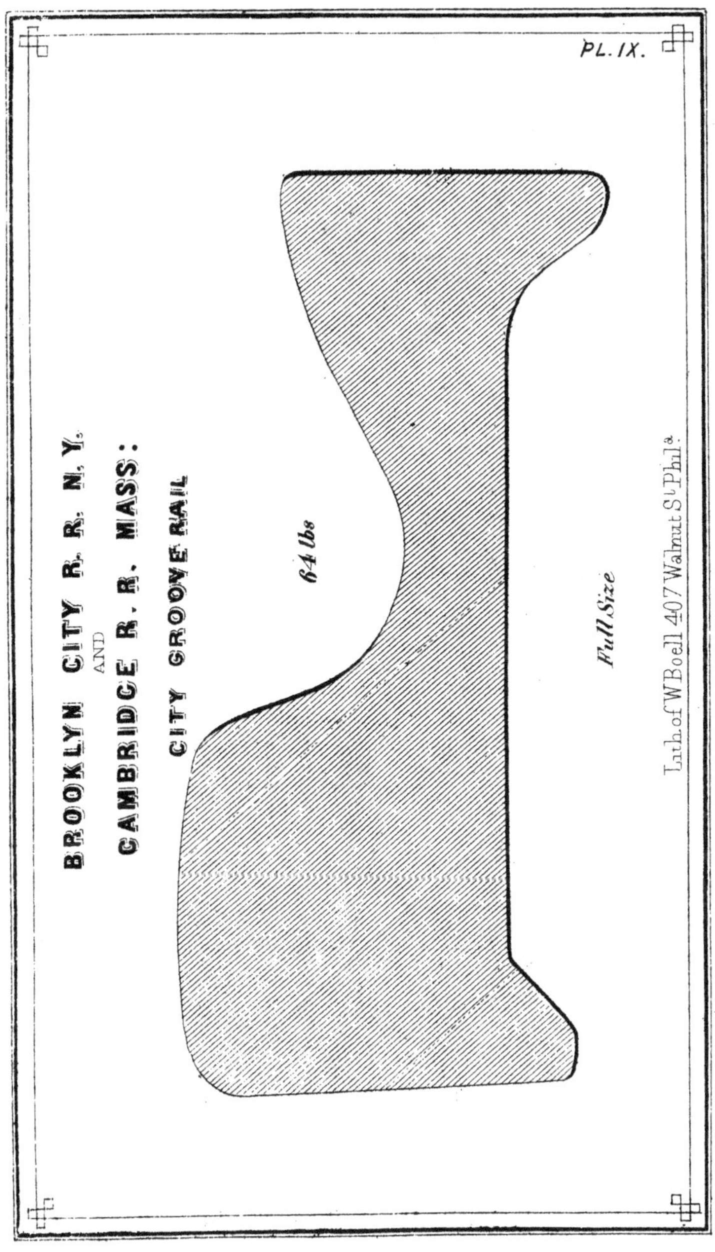
PL. IX.
BROOKLYN CITY R. R. N. Y.
AND
CAMBRIDGE R. R. MASS:
CITY GROOVE RAIL
64 lbs
Full Size
Lith. of W. Boell 407 Walnut St. Phila.

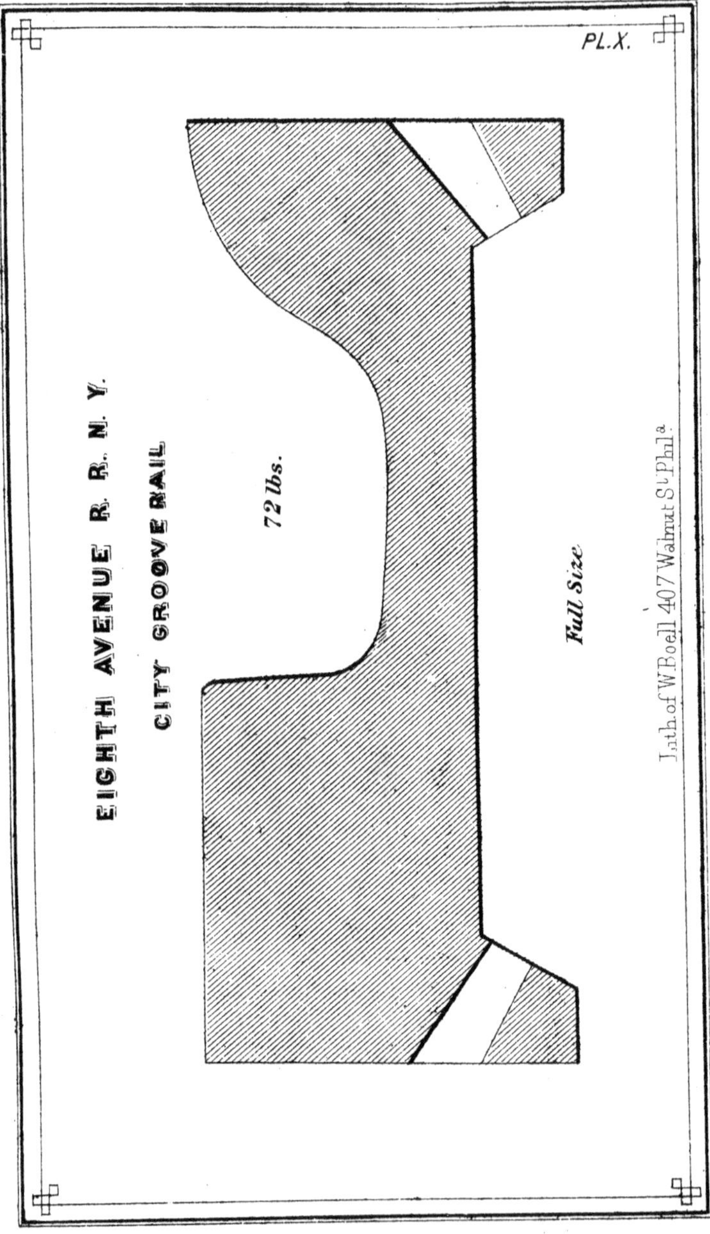
PL. X.
EIGHTH AVENUE R. R., N. Y.
CITY GROOVE RAIL
72 lbs.
Full Size
Lith. of W. Boell 407 Walnut St. Phila.

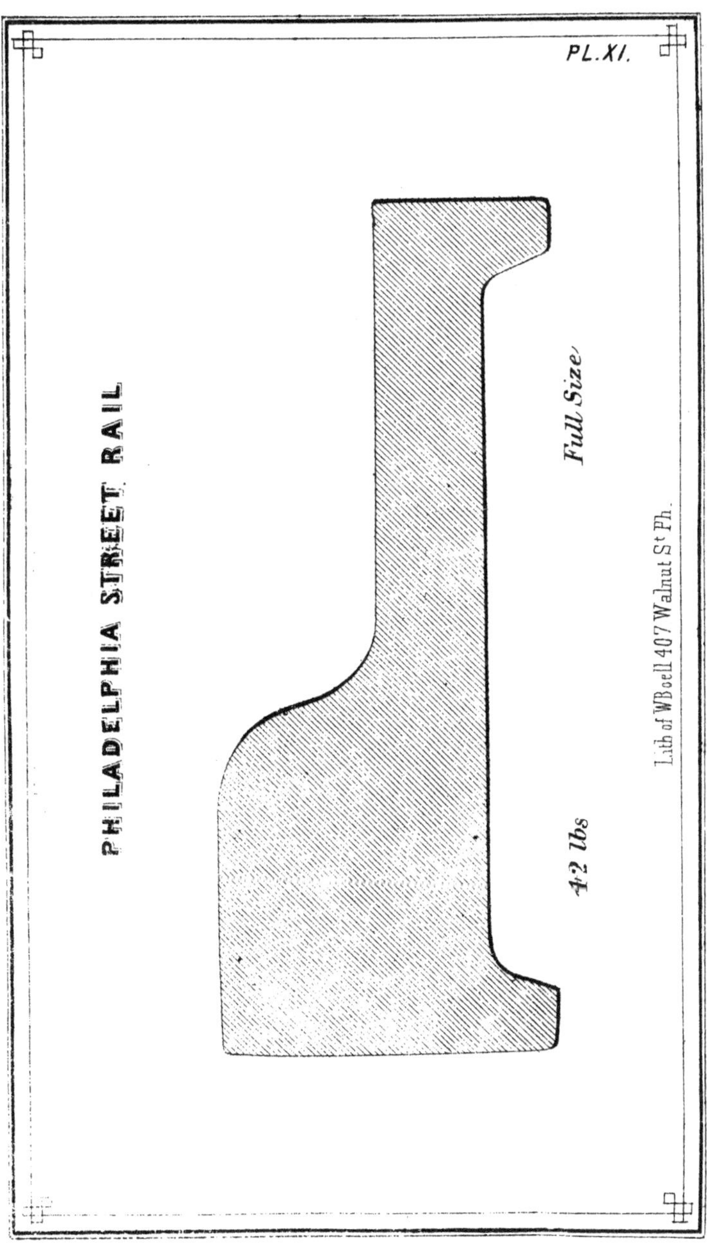
PL. XI.
PHILADELPHIA STREET RAIL
Full Size
42 lbs
Lith of W Boell 407 Walnut St Ph.

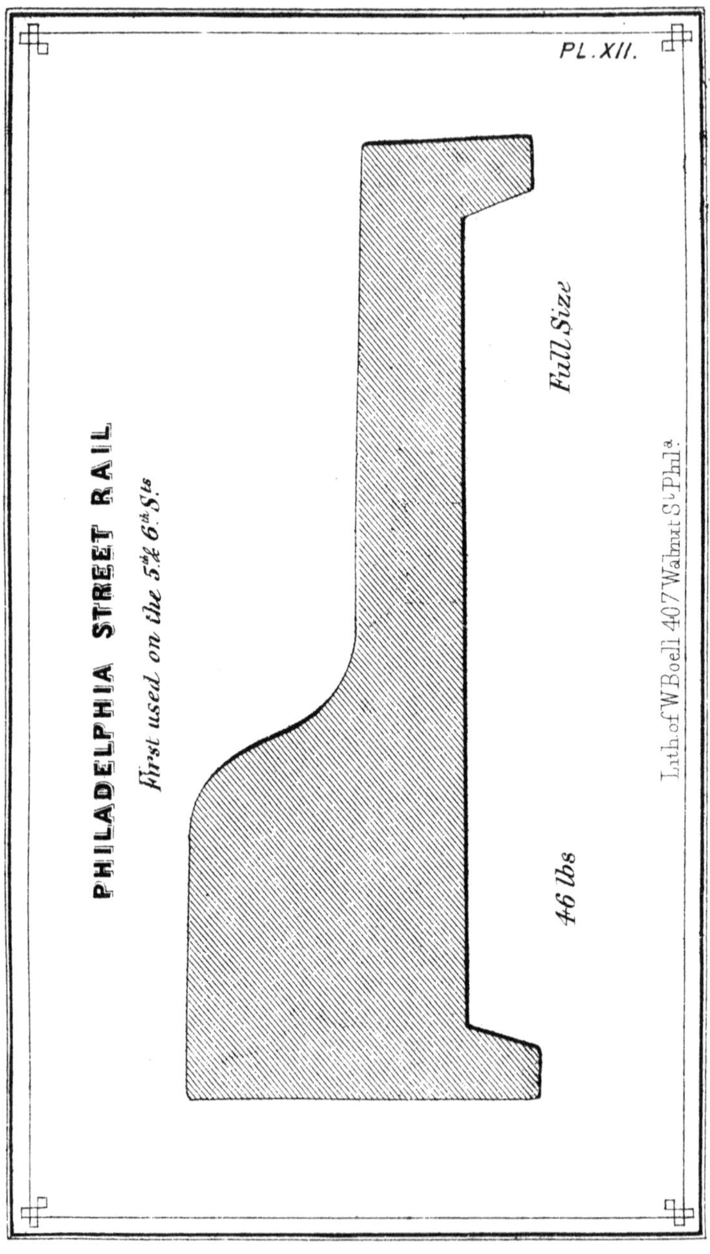
PL. XII.
PHILADELPHIA STREET RAIL
First used on the 5th & 6th Sts.
Full Size
46 lbs
Lith. of W. Boell 407 Walnut St. Phila.

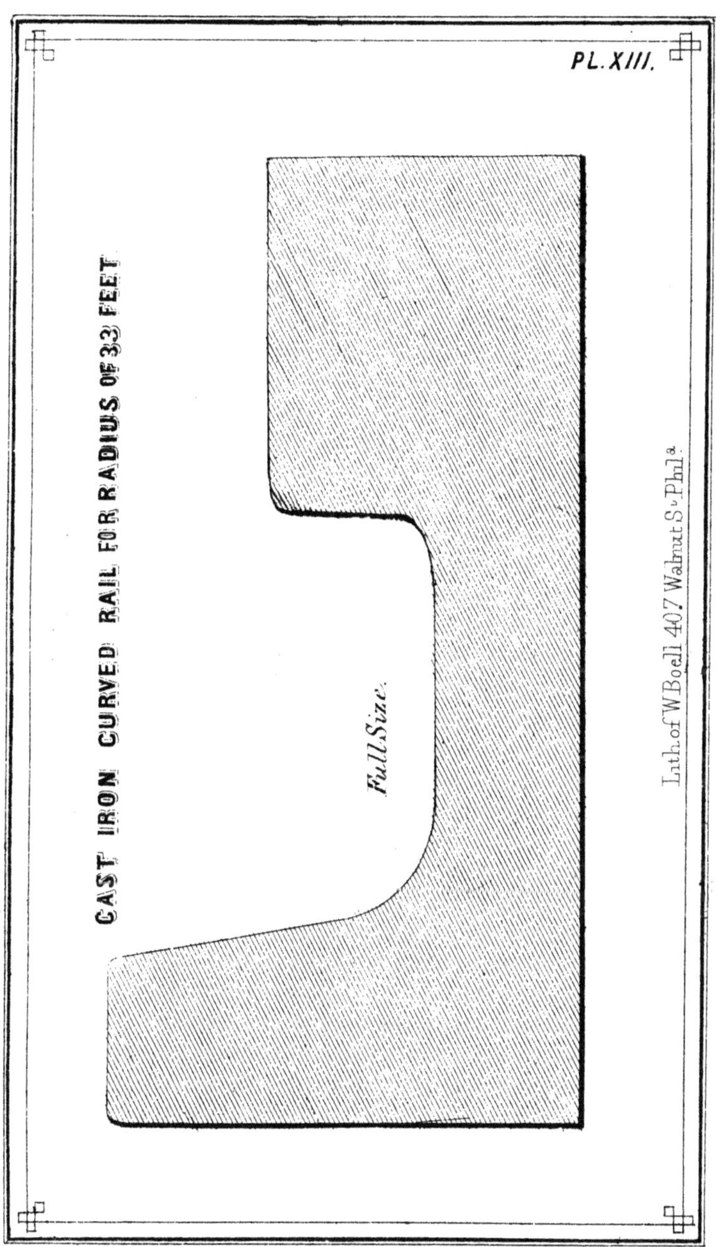
PL. XIII.
CAST IRON CURVED RAIL FOR RADIUS OF 33 FEET
Full Size.
Lith. of W. Boell 407 Walnut St. Phila.

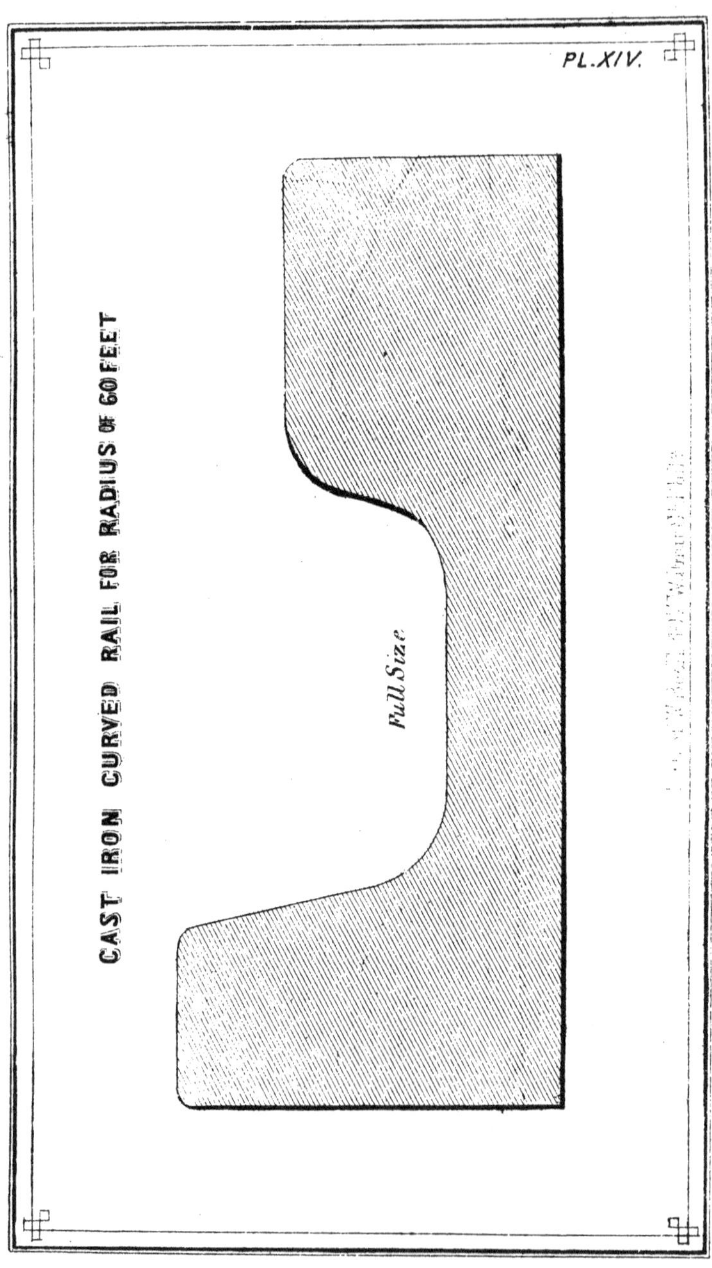
PL. XIV.
CAST IRON CURVED RAIL FOR RADIUS OF 60 FEET
Full Size

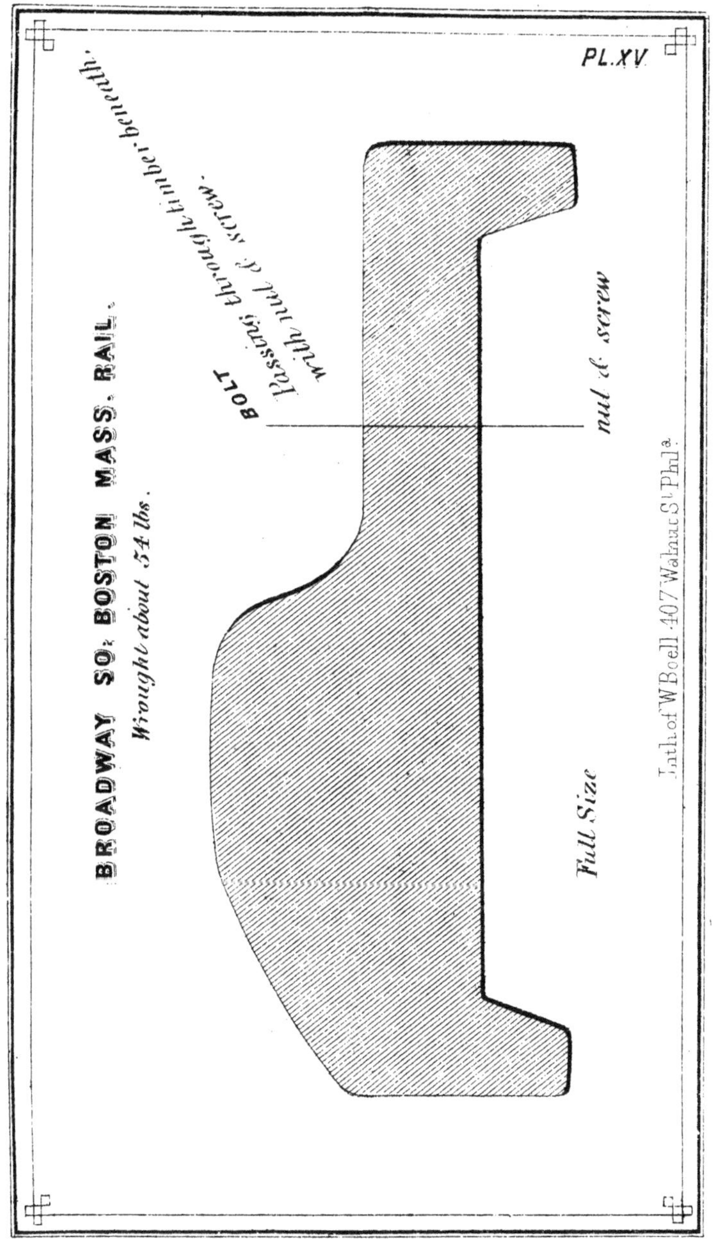
PL. XV.
BROADWAY SQ. BOSTON MASS. RAIL.
Wrought about 54 lbs.
BOLT
Passing through timber beneath
with nut & screw.
nut & screw
Full Size
Lith. of W Boell 407 Walnut St. Phila.

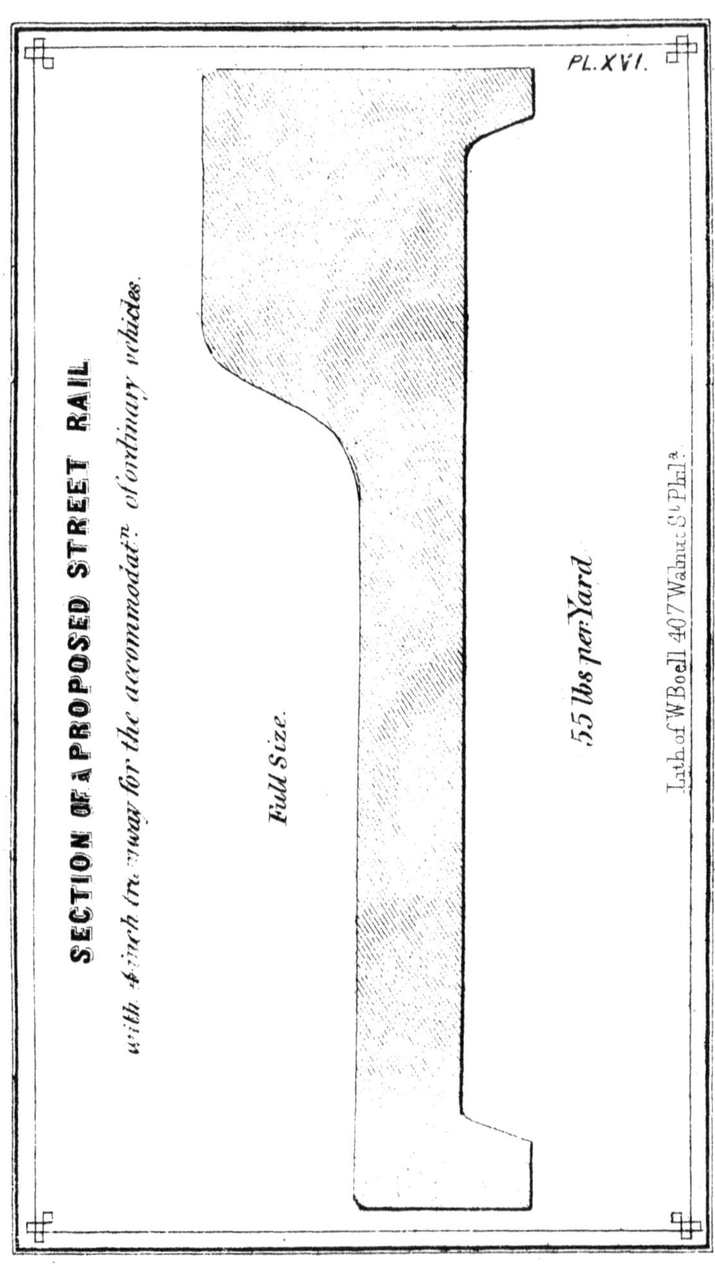
PL. XVI.
SECTION OF A PROPOSED STREET RAIL
with 4 inch tramway for the accommodatn. of ordinary vehicles.
Full Size.
55 lbs per Yard
Lith. of W Boell 407 Walnut St. Phila.

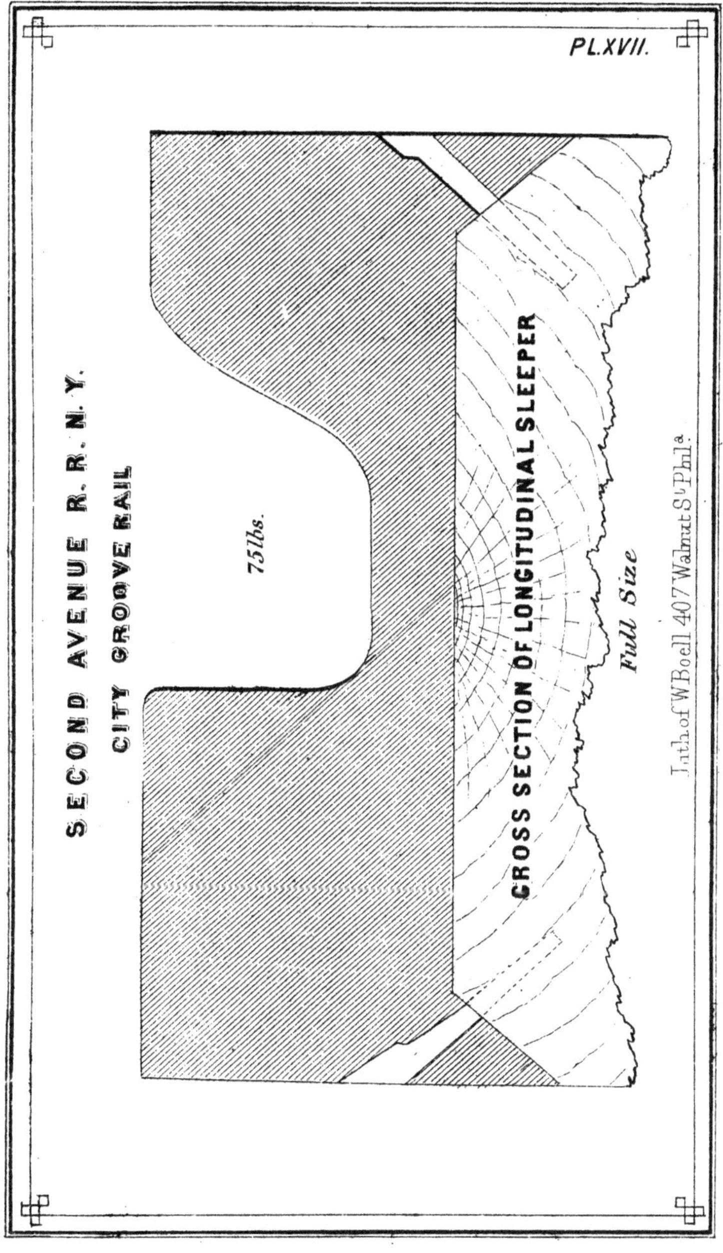
PL.XVII.
SECOND AVENUE R. R. N. Y.
CITY GROOVE RAIL
75lbs.
CROSS SECTION OF LONGITUDINAL SLEEPER
Full Size
Lith. of W. Boell 407 Walnut St Phila.

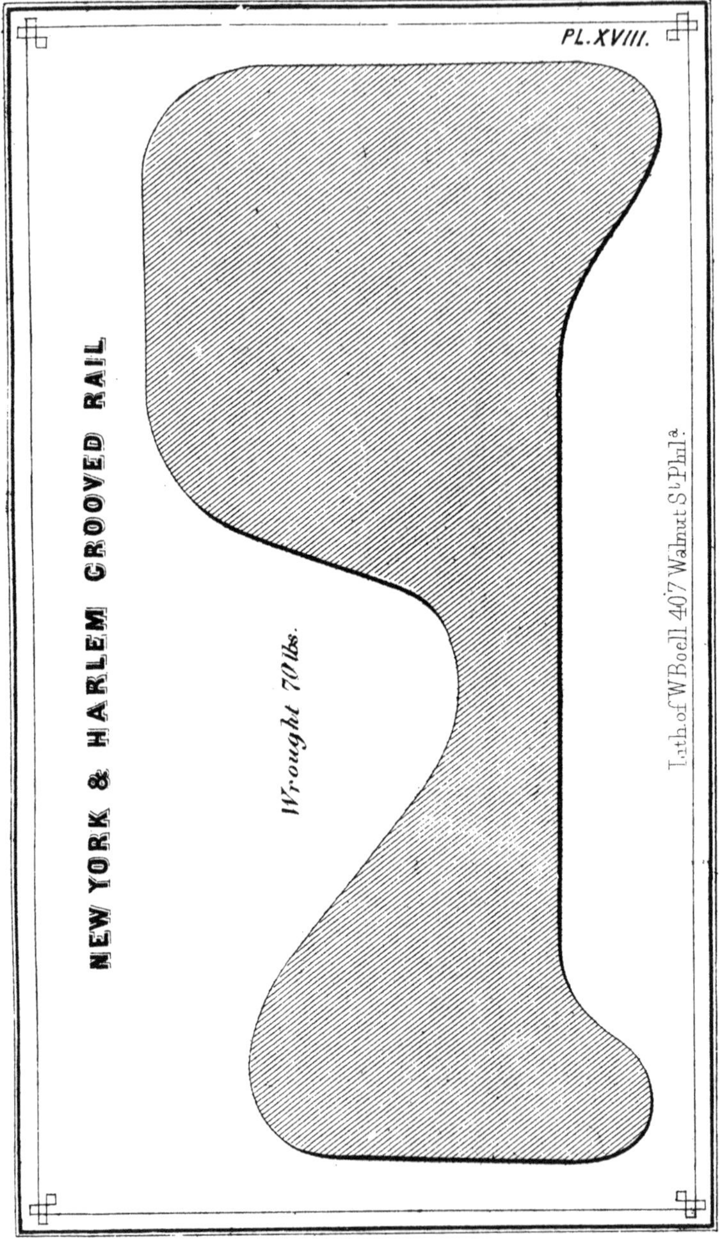
PL. XVIII.
NEW YORK & HARLEM GROOVED RAIL
Wrought 70 lbs.
Lith. of W. Boell 407 Walnut St. Phila.

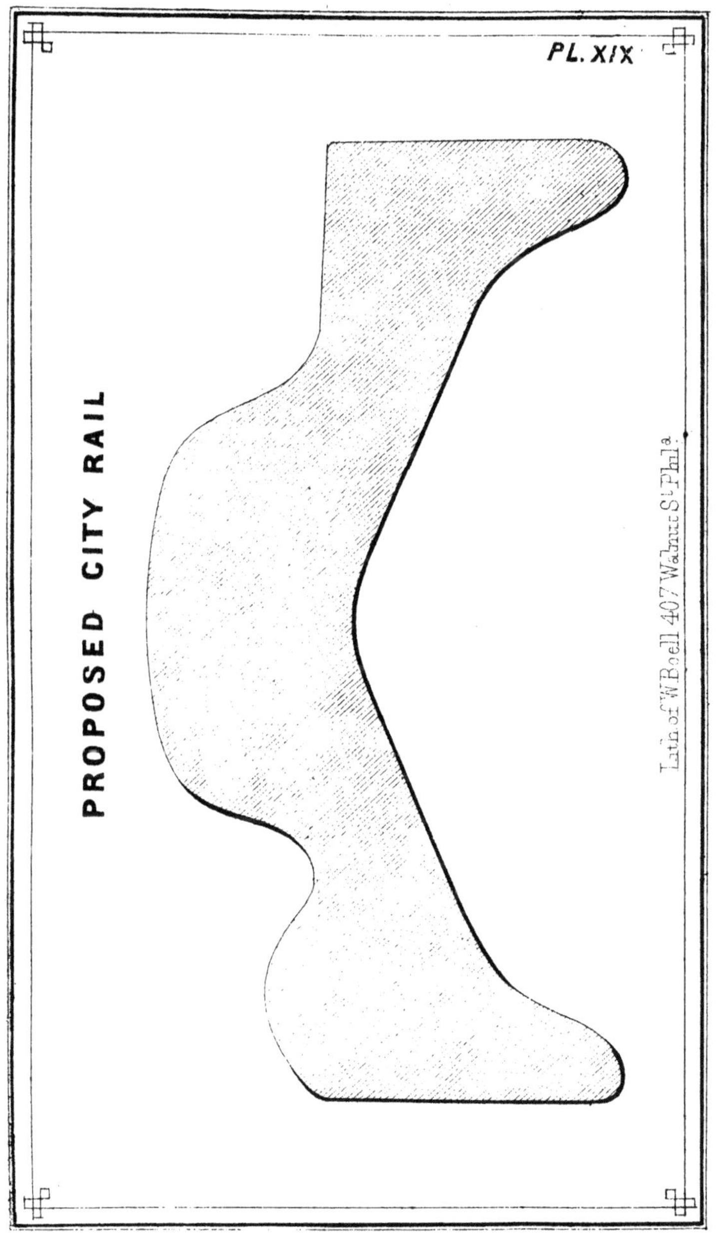
PL. XIX
PROPOSED CITY RAIL
Lith. of W. Boell 407 Walnut St. Phila.

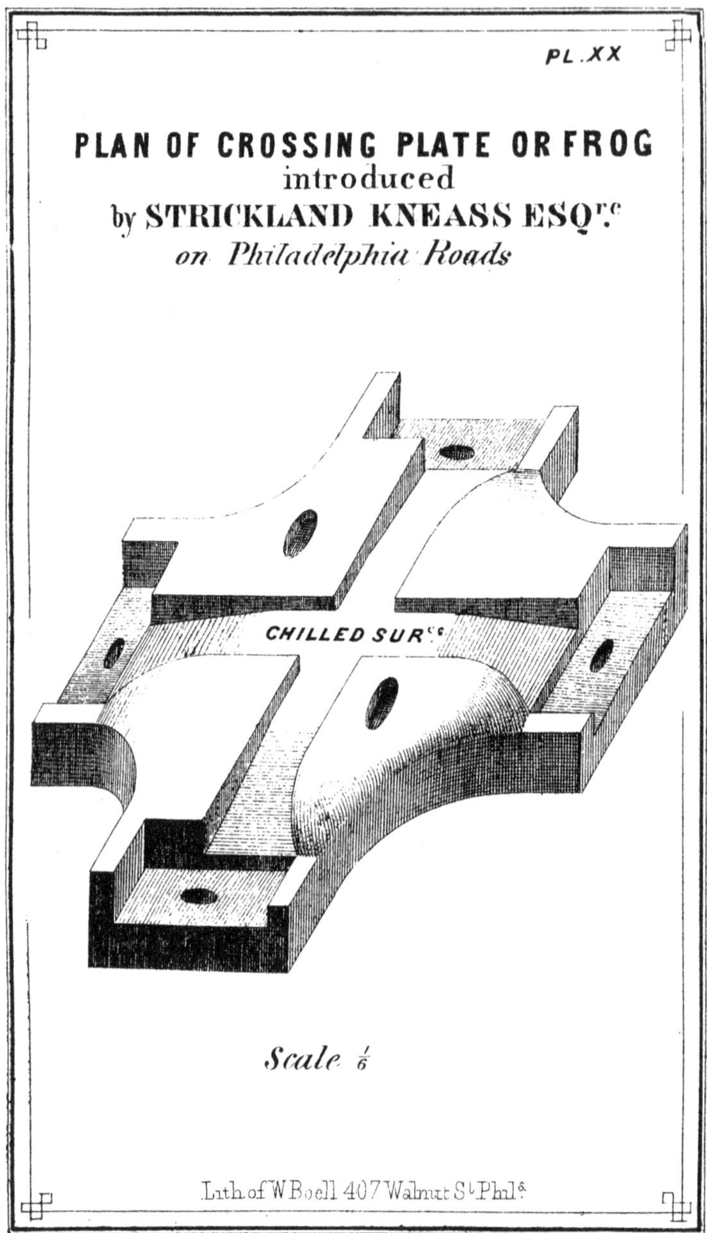
PL. XX
PLAN OF CROSSING PLATE OR FROG
introduced
by STRICKLAND KNEASS ESQ.re
on Philadelphia Roads
CHILLED SUR.ce
Scale 1/6
Lith of W Boell 407 Walnut St. Phila.

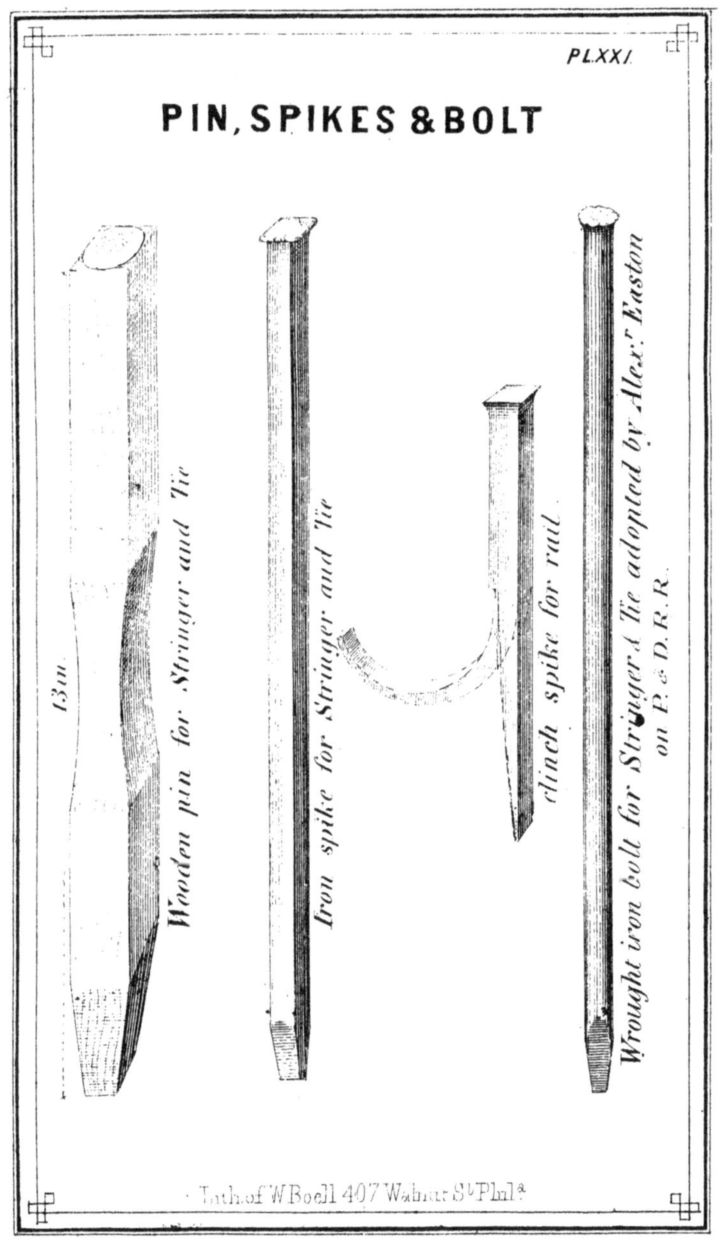
PL.XXI.
PIN, SPIKES & BOLT
13 in.
Wooden pin for Stringer and Tie
Iron spike for Stringer and Tie
clinch spike for rail.
Wrought iron bolt for Stringer & Tie adopted by Alexr. Easton on P. & D. R. R.
Lith. of W Boell 407 Walnut St. Phila.

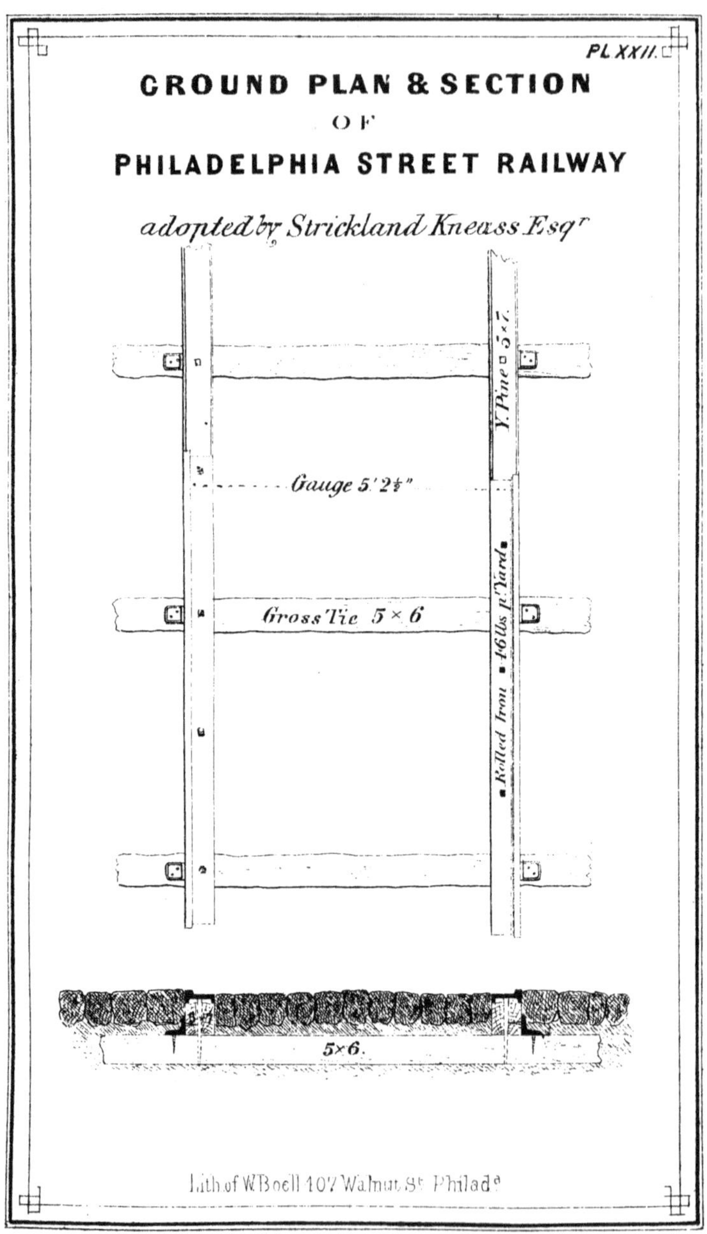
PL. XXII.
GROUND PLAN & SECTION
OF
PHILADELPHIA STREET RAILWAY
adopted by Strickland Kneass Esqr
Y. Pine 5×7.
Gauge 5' 2½"
Rolled Iron 46lbs pr Yard
Cross Tie 5 × 6
5×6.
Lith. of W. Boell 107 Walnut St. Philada

PL. XXIII

THE "HADDON" CAR

Designed for the Camden & Haddonfield Passenger Railway

by

Alexander Easton.

Litho. & Print. of W. Boell 311 Walnut St. Ph.

PL. XXIIII

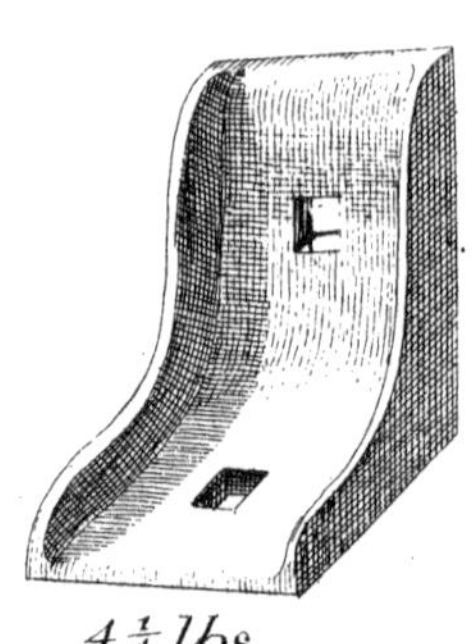

4 1/4 lbs.

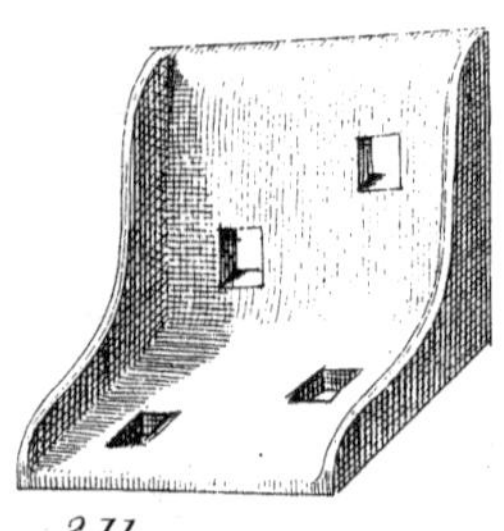

3 lbs.

2 lbs

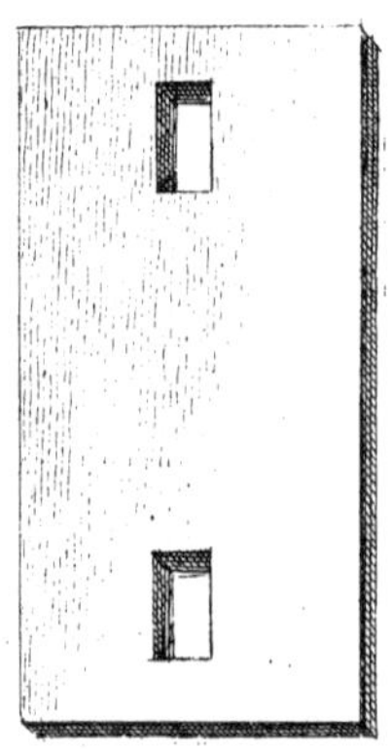

2 lbs.

CHAPTER IV.

After it has been resolved to construct a railway, it is necessary to obtain the support of competent persons, whose business habits and local importance will enable them to conciliate opposition, secure Legislative influence, and to obtain authority to incorporate a Company for its construction.

The General Assembly of Pennsylvania, in granting such official act or charter, concedes to any five or more of the commissioners named therein, full power to open books and receive subscriptions to the capital stock of such company, where and when they may deem fit; where any two or more of them, after having given due public notice thereof, shall attend, and furnish to all persons duly qualified, who shall offer to subscribe, an opportunity of so doing; the books to be kept open six hours a day for three days; no subscription being valid unless the party, at the time of subscribing, shall pay five dollars on each share. When ten per cent. of the capital stock shall be thus subscribed, the acting commissioners certifying to such fact; the Governor of the State will, by letters patent, constitute the subscribers a body corporate, under the title designated by the special Act of Assembly.

After having obtained letters patent, the commissioners are required to appoint a meeting of the subscribers or stockholders to organize the company, who shall elect, by a majority of the votes present, a President and Directors, to conduct and manage the affairs of the company.

It is of great importance that the election should devolve upon men of the highest business talent, having a pecuniary interest at stake in the prosperity of the road, with such a position in society as shall place their conduct as far as possible above impugnment.

The directors of street railways are usually entirely ignorant of the details of the matters over which they have authority; and even if it were otherwise, they could not personally superintend the works under their charge. The purchase of material not unfrequently excites some feeling in the board; as seats have been secured in railway directories that the parties holding them might serve those with whom they were connected. Experience has proved, that it is best in every respect to let the formation of the line and purchase of material to contractors, who engage to complete the work, according to certain specifications, at a stipulated price per mile; and to appoint a competent engineer to take general charge and be responsible for the construction.

The practice of misapplying capital for the payment of dividends, and the charging of current expenses to the account of capital, cannot be too strongly condemned. Cases have occurred where the future profitable working of roads has been endangered for years under this system,—which, however suitable it may be for the convenience of speculators, is fatal to the interests of those who invest permanently. The practice usually adopted to guard against this and similar abuses, is to open the accounts to the periodical inspection of shareholders; but its advantages are illusory,—for to thoroughly understand the complicated accounts of a railway, requires a thorough knowledge of the system in which they are kept, and an elaborate examination, which is a work of time, but all of which is susceptible of being simplified.

The treasurer should make up, once in three months, a blank form of report, showing the condition of the company's affairs, finance, and business; and this, not by any process of calculation of what might have been, or what it may be estimated will be; *but from actual receipts and expenses* let the exact profit be ascertained, the amount carried to profit and loss account, and all the expense accounts closed ready for another quarter's business. Let each director be supplied with a copy of such report, as is done on the Union Railway, Boston, where the practice originated, and which—under the charge of its efficient officers—is productive of the most beneficial results.

Managers of railways have had under consideration many plans by which to secure to the company all the money received by the conductors; the index, the spy, and the ticket system have each in their turn been adopted: where the latter has been systematically carried out, it has to a great extent conduced to the benefit of the company, but a certain amount of cash fares must inevitably be received by the conductor, and it is generally conceded that the interests of the company demand that the conductor shall be selected with especial reference to previous character; and on some roads he is required to get two persons known to the officers of the company to come forward and sign bonds for $500 for his faithfulness and honesty; the experience of the companies who have adopted this plan is that they have as good conductors as can be found, and that instances of dishonesty are very rare.

In the equipment of a railway, it will be true economy to provide ample means without extravagance: and in its practical management, to give adequate remuneration to competent officers and employees, without prodigality and without parsimony.

Let the purchase of equipment be guided by a judicious consideration of the local requirements of the business, instead of blindly following the custom adopted by other companies. In the construction of cars, the proportion of the paying weight to the dead weight, although in some instances is not excessive, in many others is succeptible of material modification and economy.

The two horse cars now in use weigh about two tons, and accommodate twenty passengers, although their capacity is much greater. If the time table is judiciously arranged and a correct tabular return made of the number of passengers who travel at certain hours, it will be found that there is an increased travel during certain portions of the day, and that although the larger cars may be indispensable for the heavy travel, the whole business of the intervening hours may be easily accommodated by the interspersion of light one horse cars, requiring but half the complement of men and horses. Under this arrangement, a road which employs constantly sixty, two horse cars may accommodate an equal number of passengers, at an annual saving of $40,000 in the accounts of wages and horse keep, independent of a large saving of interest and cost for maintenance of way. This system has been introduced very successfully on the Sixth Avenue Railway, New York, and in other lines the example may be followed with corresponding benefit.

The cars as now constructed are not adapted to the summer travel, being unnecessarily heavy, and too close when filled with passengers. If the roof and sides, to the bottom of the windows, were removed and a light awning supported by gas pipes, substituted, with wire work for the back and seats instead of the heavy wood work now in use: a new style of car would be introduced, the weight of which, with lighter wheels, may be reduced 2,000 lbs. Its capacity would be equal to that of the present car, and it would afford better accommodation, whilst its economy of motive power would be equal to that required to haul a constant load of fourteen passengers.

The economy of the light car may be estimated thus: A railway whose length is five miles runs thirty cars, and each car performs fourteen half trips daily, carrying fourteen passengers each way, (the number equal to the dead weight of car,) suppose the actual cost of motive power alone for carrying each passenger be estimated at two cents the half trip, then $30 \times 14 \times 14 \times 2 =$ $117 60, the actual cost per day of motive power alone for hauling excess of weight of cars. This subject is worthy the attention of the managers of railways, and particularly those whose principal business is comprised of excursion parties, &c., in the summer season. The cars should be constantly and minutely examined, and any imperfection should be immediately repaired.

Extraordinary care and vigilance in the management of the horses will result in corresponding advantages. The stables should be well ventilated and drained, and be kept constantly clean: regularity in food and work is strongly recommended. On the Sixth Avenue Railway, New York, of three hundred and ninety-three horses and mules, only three were lost (and these by accident) in one year, and eighty of this number have been in the service of the company, day and night, for six years. Mules and small Canadian horses are recommended as being more hardy, surer-footed, and less liable to casualties. The system of grinding all feed has been generally adopted: the hay is cut by horse power. In the best-managed stables, eight pounds of hay with thirteen pounds of corn and oats, ground, is the daily allowance for each horse.

The old method of making horse-shoes is being superseded by machinery, and they are now manufactured and sold at a slight advance on the cost of iron,—amounting to less than that generally allowed in blacksmiths' shops, for wastage.

From the time a road is finished, proper care should be taken to keep it up in good condition; and upon the proper attention paid to this, will depend, in a great measure, the ultimate cost of repairs. For this purpose an intelligent foreman, with sufficient assistance, should be permanently employed; ditches should be constantly cleaned, but without being widened or deepened; the horse-way should be kept free from standing water; depressions in the rail, however slight, must be raised from the foundation, and the greatest care taken that the track is always accurately gauged.

The durability of rails is dependent, mainly, on the amount of traffic upon them; and on street rails, the continued action of the brake and sand and dirt, so liable to accumulate, have a very injurious effect: this latter difficulty may be partially overcome by placing a small broom in front of each wheel, and an economy of motive power thereby effected.

It is difficult to estimate the duration of cross-ties, as this will depend not upon the amount of work done on the road, but upon the quality of the timber and the vicissitudes of moisture and temperature to which they may be exposed. It is the result of experience that the superstructure of a railway does not decay and wear uniformly,—that some portions require to be replaced from year to year, whilst others remain perfect for six, seven, or eight years; and in the course of eight or nine years, under a judicious system of repairs, the whole of the timber will have been replaced.

In establishing rates of fare on suburban roads some difficulty is at first experienced; on these roads the ticket system, when properly conducted, will be found productive of great advantages, and invariably, to please the passengers who form the permanent travel. Cards explaining the rates of way-fares, defining with distinctness the points designated, should be conspicuously posted in the waiting-rooms and cars. The following is a copy of The Union Railway Company's rates of fare, with the reduction made in the sale of tickets, which, however, are only sold in strips of one or two dollars' worth :—

RATES OF FARE.

For convenience in determining the Rates of Fare upon the Cambridge, Waltham, and Watertown, and Newton Railroads, the various portions of each of the roads will hereafter be known by the following names:—

Boston—From Bowdoin Square to the junction of the East Cambridge road at Court street.

Cambridgeport—From Court street to Dana street, and from the junction of Main and River streets to the centre of the draw on the bridge leading to Brighton.

Cambridge—From Dana street to Harvard Square, from thence to Fayerweather street on the Mount Auburn road, and from Harvard Square to the terminus of the North Avenue Branch.

Mount Auburn—From Fayerweather street to the terminus of the Cambridge Railroad at the bridge.

Watertown—From the Railroad bridge to the terminus of the road in Watertown centre.

Union Square—From the centre of the draw on the bridge to Union Hall.

Cattle Fair—From Union Hall to Foster street.

Brighton—From Foster street to the terminus of the Newton Railroad.

RATES OF CASH FARE.

	Cash.	Tickets.
Between any point in Boston and Court street, Cambridgeport, or East Cambridge,	5 cts.	None.
" " and Cambridgeport, above Court street,	10 "	16 for $1
" " and Cambridge,	10 "	12 " 1
" " and Mount Auburn,	15 "	10 " 1
" " and Watertown,	15 "	8 " 1
" " and Union Square,	10 "	25 " 2
" " and Cattle Fair,	15 "	10 " 1
" " and Brighton,	15 "	8 " 1

WAY FARE.

In Boston,	5 cts.
Between Cambridgeport and any point in Cambridge,	5 "
" " and any point in Brighton,	6 "
" " and any point in Mount Auburn,	10 "
" " and any point in Watertown,	12 "
" the junction at Court street and any point in East Cambridge,	3 "

CHILDREN, BETWEEN FOUR AND TWELVE YEARS OF AGE.

Between Boston and any point in Cambridgeport and Cambridge,	5 cts.
" " and any point in Mount Auburn,	8 "
" " and any point in Watertown,	10 "
" " and any point in Brighton,	10 "
Local Fare,	3 "

In no case whatever will passengers be permitted to ride in one car, and then leave the car and continue on to their final destination in the next or any succeeding car, without paying IN EACH CAR full fare for the distance traveled in that car according to the above schedule of rates.

Baggage.—An additional fare will be charged for each trunk, box, or other parcel.

The number of employees, and their classification, on a railway, whose equipment consists of thirty-five cars and two hundred and fifty-one horses, is as follows:—

President,	1	Drivers,	28
Treasurer,	1	Mechanics in Car-shop,	3
Superintendent,	1	Harness-maker,	1
Treasurer's Clerk,	1	Blacksmiths,	9
Superintendent's Clerk,	1	Watchmen,	5
Overseers of Stables,	4	Hostlers,	24
Conductors,	29	Switchmen,	7
Starters,	2	Roadmen,	7
Persons regularly employed,			124

In the appointment of officers and employees great care should be taken to select those only who can establish their merit upon undisputed qualifications,—the proof of which does not always exist in the long list of signatures appended to an application.

It is of vital importance that the superintendent should be a man of high moral character, decisive and energetic: an extensive discretionary power should be allowed him. The salary should be so apportioned as to secure the desired qualifications.

The whole operative department should be under the

control of the superintendent, who will be responsible for the safe and regular transportation of passengers, make daily returns to the treasurer of all moneys received, and other duties more fully explained in the by-laws which may be adopted. Every possible precaution should be taken for the prevention of accidents, by establishing rules *applicable* to the duties required, and enforcing a strict observance of them. The following list of accidents on various roads is given, as showing the causes from which they most generally arise.

On one road the number of passengers carried in one year being over eight millions, only five sustained personal injury—three by jumping off while the car was in motion; one by sitting on the steps of the car when crossing the trench of a sewer, and one by collision with a hook and ladder truck, while standing on the front platform.

Two children, who ran under the horses, were knocked down and injured.

One man found lying on the track in the night time, intoxicated, was killed; and another, under the same circumstances, lost his arm.

One man, doubtless intoxicated, threw himself under the horses, and was killed.

A strict investigation was made in each of these cases, and resulted in exonerating the employees of the company from all blame.

A passenger on Hamilton Avenue car got off on account of cold feet, and ran along side, holding on to the guard. Was warned by the driver of the danger, but persisted. His foot slipped and was caught by the wheel and crushed. The passenger admitted that he alone was to blame.

A passenger on car 17, fell off the front platform, at the corner of Myrtle and Carlton Avenues, and before the car could be stopped, the wheel passed over his leg. Was taken to the hospital, where he died. Verdict of coroner's jury, "Died from injuries received by accidentally falling from and being run over by car 17."

A boy, two years old, was run over by car 75, and died from the injuries received. The child ran directly under the horses. The car was going slow and was stopped as soon as possible. The coroner's jury exonerated the conductor and driver from blame.

A child, six years old, ran suddenly from behind another car directly against the hind leg of one of the horses of car No. 30, near the corner of Fulton avenue and Smith street, was run over and killed. Verdict of coroner's jury, "Accidentally killed."

A boy, nine years old, a passenger on car 43, jumped off the forward platform and fell. The wheel passed over his arm, crushing it badly.

A boy, seven years old, was run over and killed by one of two vacant cars which were being taken to the repair shop, at the corner of Sands street and Hudson avenue, but in what manner is not known, as no person saw it, and the driver had no knowledge of the transaction. It was about 8 o'clock P. M. Verdict of the coroner's jury, "accidental death." The father of the boy was present and acquitted the company from blame.

A boy, run over at Fifty-fourth street—injured in leg by wheel. Since recovered.

A man lying on the track at Forty-third street—run over by front wheel—sent to hospital and arm amputated. Intoxicated.

A man, in jumping off the car in Division street, fell and wheel passed over his foot.

A man was run over by a car at 1 A. M., at Fifty-sixth street. He was grossly intoxicated, and was lying in the track; it being very dark was not seen by driver—had been taken from the track a short time previous—sent to hospital, where he died from the injuries he received.

A man, while in a state of intoxication, in attempting to get on a car at Sixty-fifth street, fell under the horses and was run over by the cars. He died in five minutes.

A young man about twenty years of age, (intoxicated) attempted to step from the forward platform of a car when in motion, near Porters, on Washington street, lost his balance and fell. One of the wheels of the car passed over his leg, crushing the bones. He was taken to the hospital, and the limb was amputated the next day. He died the following day.

A boy ten years of age, was instantly killed by being run over by a Mt. Pleasant car, near Dover street.

An intoxicated man was run over by a car on Washington, near Springfield street—hand slightly injured.

A boy about eight years of age, ran from the rear of an inward bound car, directly under the horses of an outward bound car, was run over and somewhat injured.

A man attempted to alight from the forward platform of a car when in motion, was knocked down by the corner of the car and had his foot crushed by the wheel.

A child was knocked down by the horses of a car on Tremont street. No serious injury.

A blacksmith, in the employment of the company, stepped from the forward platform of a car while in motion, and in falling, injured his arm.

APPENDIX.

The duties of Conductors and Drivers cannot be too plainly worded, and should be always strictly enforced. A printed copy should be posted in a conspicuous place in each Car: the following, it is believed, combine all that can be necessary.

RULES AND REGULATIONS FOR CONDUCTORS,

ADOPTED BY THE UNION RAILWAY COMPANY, BOSTON.

1. You will not be allowed on duty without the Official badge.

2. The Driver and car will be under your direction while on duty.

3. You will be particular to start on time, and keep so, as near as possible.

4. Your watch must be kept exact with the clock at the Superintendent's Office.

5. You must be in readiness to render the Driver assistance in all places where it is necessary to detach the horses from the car; and not allow the car to move unless you are at the brake on the *front* platform.

6. Extra cars must be kept out of the way of all Regular cars.

7. You will request passengers to get off and on the car at the rear end, and on the side nearest the sidewalk, to prevent accidents.

8. You must be particular and not start your car until a passenger is fairly received or landed.

9. You will be civil and attentive to passengers,—giving proper assistance to ladies and children.

10. All accidents and collisions must be reported immediately on arrival at the Office, with names and residences of persons witnessing the same. If any are injured, render all the assistance possible.

11. You will be held responsible for any misconduct or carelessness of your Driver while on Duty, unless reported immediately at the Office.

12. The Driver will depend entirely upon the bell as a signal for starting; and he will not be allowed to start without such "SIGNAL."

13. You will not allow any smoking in the car or upon the platforms.

14. All obstructions upon the track, such as broken wagons, sleds, sleighs, &c., must be reported to the nearest agent of the road as soon as possible; also at the Office. The car must not be taken from the track to go round such obstructions if it can be avoided.

15. In case of fire on the line of the road, you will send for the Hose Bridges, which are kept at the 'Port and at Dunster-Street Stables.

16. You must not allow children to take hold of the car, to run with or beside it, to make or play carriage of it.

17. When in Boston, you *must not leave the car*, but see that proper attention is shown to passengers, and provide seats for as many as possible.

18. The inward car has the right to the road on all the single track.

19. Running time from	Cambridge to Boston,	3	miles,	25 min.
"	Cambridge to North Avenue,	1	"	8 "
"	" Mount Auburn,	1½	"	12 "
"	" Watertown,	4	"	25 "

RULES AND REGULATIONS FOR DRIVERS,

ADOPTED BY THE UNION RAILWAY COMPANY, BOSTON.

1. You must be on duty promptly at the time.

2. You must start your horses by the bell.

3. You must keep a sharp look-out for your horses, and for persons who may wish to enter the car; must not *look back into the car*, but depend upon the bell as a signal for starting.

4. You must come to a full stop for *all* persons who wish to enter the car, unless the bell strikes for you to go on.

5. You will request passengers to get on and off the car at the rear end, and on the side nearest the sidewalk, to prevent accidents: and be particular to bring the rear end of your car to the flagging.

6. You will be civil to passengers, teamsters, or other persons who may be in your way or on the track; you must speak pleasantly and politely, requesting them to move.

7. You must notify the Conductor by striking the bell when there are passengers on the front end of the car who have not paid their fare.

8. You must walk your horses around all short curves, such as that in Harvard Square, and not stop upon them. Also walk your horses over the switches at the 'Port stables.

9. You must not allow any person to drive your horses or tend your brake, but those employed by the Company.

10. You must not, under any circumstances whatever, leave your horses when attached to the car, without a responsible person to hold them.

11. In all places where the street is dug open for paving, or other purposes, so as to endanger the safety of your horses, they must be detached from the car.

12. You must never detach your horses from the car when it is in motion, unless the Conductor is with you on the front of the car.

13. When in Boston, you must look out for carriages coming in from the cross streets, and drive slow, not exceeding five miles per hour, at any point. And when coming down the hill, past North Russell street, not to exceed three miles per hour. If two or more cars are obliged to wait at the foot of the hill, they must keep at least one hundred feet apart, and never stop in front of a cross street.

14. You must not let your horses "gallop" up the hill.

15. You must know positively that the Draw on the Bridge is on, and all-right before you drive upon it.

16. You will be held responsible for damage done to your car by your carelessness.

17. You must not allow boys to get on the front end of the car without coming to a full stop.

18. You must walk your horses past the several School-houses, on the line of the road, when the children are playing in the street.

19. You must not start from Boston, or from the Office, without the signal of the bell by the Conductor, or some other authorized person.

20. When you meet or pass any procession, Fire or Military Company, you must drive very slow. Should there be a Fire Engine attached to the car, your rate of speed must not exceed five miles per hour.

21. You must keep the outside of your car clean.

22. You must notify the Conductor when passengers are smoking on the front platform.

Rules adopted by the Second Avenue Railroad Company, N. Y.

1. The Conductor shall stand *with his back to the cars,* and shall give his attention to looking for passengers, seating them and collecting fares, and avoid all unnecessary conversation.

2. He shall be civil and attentive to all passengers, giving especial attention to ladies, children, and elderly persons, while getting in and out of the car, and as far as possible shall provide seats for all persons on the car.

3. He shall request passengers in leaving the car to pass out of the rear door, and from the side of the door which is opposite the other track.

4. He shall keep on his time as nearly as possible, and shall report every detention, with the cause thereof, to the Starting Agent, at the terminus at which he first arrives.

5. He shall see that his driver turns the curves on a walk, and *communicate with his Driver by means of the bell only*, striking the bell twice for the Driver to proceed faster, and three times to proceed slower.

6. He shall permit no smoking on any part of the car, and shall politely inform any person in the act of smoking on the car, that it is against the rules of the Company.

7. He shall allow no intoxicated person to enter the car, or ride on the platform.

8. When any accident or collision occurs, he shall endeavor to obtain the names and residences of the witnesses to the same, and shall immediately report them, with the cause and extent of such accident, to the Superintendent or Receiver, at Forty-second street.

9. He shall obey the orders of the Starting Agent at each end of the route.

10. He shall deposit all articles left in the car with the Receiver, at Forty-second street.

11. He shall not allow any person to ride on the car without paying fare, except firemen in uniform passing to or from a fire, or policemen who ride on the platform. Employees of the Company who ride must pay fare.

12. He shall call out, in passing, the streets named in the Time Table, and all streets at which passengers inform him that they desire to get out.

13. He shall collect fare for trunks, and all large or heavy parcels.

14. The *Drivers are to obey the Conductors' orders:* and, in case of neglect to do so, the Conductor shall immediately report them to the Superintendent.

15. Conductors and Drivers that drink any intoxicating liquors when on duty, will be discharged.

16. Conductors, upon making their returns, must report the condition of their car, and any repairs necessary on the track, to the Receiver.

Rules adopted by the Sixth Avenue Railway, N. Y.

1. You will not *permit smoking* in or about your car, nor any person to get on or off through the front gates.

2. You will not sit in your car, or on the platform railing, while on duty, nor do anything whereby your attention may be drawn from duty. Avoid all unnecessary conversation, and keep diligent look-out for persons wishing to ride.

3. You will keep on time as near as possible, and see that your Driver walks his horses or mules round all curves, and does not drive nearer the car a-head than one block.

4. You will report accidents or collisions at the Superintendent's Office at Forty-third street, immediately on arrival, with the names and residences of witnesses. When cases require surgical attendance, call in the services of a Surgeon, whose charges for services then rendered will be recognized.

5. You will make your communication with the Driver by passing outside the car, keeping the front door closed when necessary, and will observe that the locks are kept in order.

6. You will not be allowed on duty without the official badge on your hat or cap.

7. You will obey the orders of the Starter at each end of the line.

8. You will call out the name of the cross-streets at the first cross-walk, and stop the car at the second, if requested.

9. You will request passengers to get off the car on the side nearest the side-walk, to prevent accidents from cars approaching.

10. You will be civil and attentive to passengers, giving proper assistance to ladies and children getting in or out, and never start the car before passengers are fairly received or landed.

11. You will allow no *free* riding, except in the cases hereinafter specified.

12. You will register all passengers on the Indicator the moment they enter the car. See that your Indicator is kept in order, and set by the Starter at each end of the route.

13. You will permit Directors holding "Directors' Tickets," and Employees of the road holding tickets, to pass free in all cases on their delivering to you a ticket.

14. You will accord free passage *without tickets* only to Firemen in the dress of the Fire Department.

15. You will request passengers *to have their fares ready* before stopping the car to leave.

16. You will deposit all articles of value left by passengers in the cars, with the Receiver, who will hold them at the office until reclaimed by the owners, to be returned to you at the end of six months if not so claimed.

17. You will charge all children occupying seats full fare, and children under twelve years of age three cents.

18. For the convenience of passengers, and to avoid encumbering the cars, the Conductors are directed to collect a fare for every trunk, box, basket, or package placed in the cars, too large to be held by the owners without annoyance to other passengers, and in no case to receive any such trunk, box, basket, or package, unless the same be in charge of a passenger.

Rules adopted by the Third Avenue Railway, N. Y.

1. The Conductor shall give his attention to looking for passengers and seating them, and collecting the fares, and *shall avoid all unnecessary conversation.*

2. He shall be civil and attentive to all passengers, giving *especial attention to ladies, children, and elderly persons,* while getting in and out of the car; and, as far as possible, shall provide seats for all persons on the car.

3. He shall request passengers in leaving the car to pass out of the rear door, and from the side of the car which is opposite the other track.

4. He shall keep on his time as nearly as possible, and shall report every detention of more than three minutes, with the cause thereof, to the Starting Agent, at the terminus at which he first arrives.

5. He shall wear upon his hat or cap the following badge, "Conductor Third A. R. R. C."

6. He shall permit no smoking on any part of the car, and shall politely inform any person, in the act of smoking on the car, that it is against the rules of the Company.

7. He shall allow no *person intoxicated* to enter the car, or ride on the platform.

8. When any accident or collision occurs, he shall obtain the names and residences of the witnesses of the same, and shall immediately report them, with the cause and extent of such accident, to the Receiver at the Depot.

9. He shall obey the orders of the Starting Agent at each end of the route.

10. He shall deposit all articles left in the car at the office of the Receiver.

11. He shall not allow any person to ride on the car without paying fare, except *firemen in uniform* passing to or from a fire.

12. He shall call out, in passing, the number of the wide streets, commencing with Eighth street on the passage up, and with the depot on the passage down.

13. When the car crosses Fifth, Broome, and Grand streets, he shall be in a position to avoid any collision with the cars of the Second and Fourth Avenue roads, and *shall require the Driver to pass slowly over all switches.*

14. No articles affecting the comfort or convenience of the passengers will be allowed inside the cars.

15. All articles of a bulky nature, occupying the space of a passen-

ger, will be charged *five cents;* but all such articles must be carried on the front platform.

N. B.—*Passengers* are requested to report at the Company's Office, Sixty-first street and Third Avenue, or to the Starter at the corner of Ann street, any impropriety or neglect on the part of the Conductors or Drivers.

BY-LAWS

ADOPTED BY

THE DIRECTORS OF THE SIXTH AVENUE RAILROAD, NEW YORK.

Sect. 1. The property and business of the Sixth Avenue Railroad Company shall, except when otherwise specially provided, be managed and controlled by a Board of Directors, not exceeding thirteen in number, elected from the Shareholders in the Company in the manner hereinafter prescribed. The Directors shall hold their offices until others are elected in their place, and shall have power to fill vacancies in their body, from the Shareholders, at any meeting of the Board subsequent to that at which the existence of such vacancy shall be made known. The vote of a majority of the number of Directors then existing shall be requisite to elect a Director.

Sect. 2. Stated meetings of the Shareholders for the election of Directors shall be held on the second Tuesday of January in each year, at a time and place to be fixed by resolution of the Board. Notice of the election shall be published for two weeks next preceding said election in two or more of the daily papers. The election shall be by ballot, and three Shareholders, not Directors or officers, shall be at the same time elected as inspectors, to hold the next annual election and to certify the result thereof; and in case of any vacancy amongst said inspectors, the same shall be filled by the Board of Directors.

Stated meetings of the Board of Directors shall be held on the first Thursday after the first day of each month, at the office of the Company, at eleven o'clock, A. M., or at such other time and place as the Board may, by resolution, from time to time direct. A majority of the whole number of Directors for the time being shall constitute a quorum for the transaction of business, but a less number may meet and adjourn from time to time until a quorum shall be present.

The President may call special meetings of the Directors at his discretion; he shall also call a special meeting whenever three of the Directors shall request him in writing to do so. All stated and special meetings shall be called by a written or printed notice to each Director, but no business shall be taken up or sanctioned at a special meeting except that referred to in said notice, unless with the consent of a majority of the whole Board, expressed by their votes at such meeting.

Special meetings of the Shareholders shall be called by the President, whenever requested so to do by Shareholders owning one thousand shares of stock.

The order of business of the Board of Directors shall be:—

1. The calling of the roll.
2. The reading of the minutes of the preceding meeting.
3. The reading of the minutes of the Executive Committee.
4. Communications and reports from the President.
5. Reports from the Treasurer.
6. Reports from the Superintendent.
7. Reports of Standing Committees.
8. Reports of Special Committees.
9. Unfinished business.
10. Miscellaneous business.

At a special meeting, the business for which the meeting was called shall have a preference immediately after the reading of the minutes of the Executive Committee.

All questions shall be decided by the vote of the majority of the Directors present, unless herein otherwise provided, and the yeas and nays shall be recorded on the demand of one member.

Questions relating to priority of business, motions to adjourn, to lay on the table, and to close debate and appeals from the decision of the chair on points of order, are not debatable; but the chair, in stating a decision on a point of order, may assign a reason therefor.

SECT. 3. There shall be an Executive Committee, to consist of the President and two other Directors. The said committee shall be chosen and vacancies therein filled by ballot by the Board of Directors. The committee shall fix the periods for its stated meetings, and it shall be proper for any member thereof to call the same together for special business.

All the powers and duties of the Board of Directors not herein delegated to the officers of this Company, or delegated by the Board of Directors to other committees, shall be exercised and discharged during the recess of the Board by the Executive Committee. Provided, however, that alterations and additions to the track and buildings, the purchase of cars, and the increase of the force of men, mules, and horses employed by the Company, the allowance of claims not arising under contract and *not* exceeding two hundred and fifty dollars in amount, and all sales of property, other than mules or horses and damaged provisions, are reserved for the express direction of the Board. The President and one other member shall be a quorum of said committee at any stated meeting. They shall also be a quorum at any special meeting, of which notices have been duly sent to all the members.

They shall keep regular minutes of their proceedings, which shall be read to the Board at the next ensuing meeting, and the question of approval shall then be taken thereon.

The committee shall have the power to suspend any subordinate officer from duty, and to diminish the force of men, horses, or mules, and shall be bound to report all such acts at the next ensuing meeting of the Board.

There shall be a Finance Committee, to consist of three members. The Finance Committee shall keep a general supervision over the pecuniary condition of the Company, and shall report from time to time such measures as they may deem advisable to meet the obligations and sustain the credit of the Company. It shall be their duty to examine —at least once in every month—the accounts and vouchers of all the officers of the Company.

The members of the Finance Committee shall be chosen, and vacancies filled therein, and stated and special meetings thereof called in like manner as those of the Executive Committee. They shall likewise keep regular minutes of their proceedings, and report at each stated meeting of the Board, and at such special meetings as they may have any communication, report, or suggestion to offer.

The Board of Directors may appoint other Committees, and delegate such powers to said Committees as they may deem advisable, provided that every Committee so appointed shall make a written report to the stated meetings of the Board of their proceedings for the preceding month, and oftener when required.

SECT. 4. The principal Officers of the Company shall be a President, a Treasurer, a Secretary, and a Superintendent. The Board of Directors may also appoint a Receiver, an Assistant Receiver, a Book-keeper, and such other officers, clerks and assistants, as they may from time to time deem necessary.

They may, in their discretion, invest either of the principal officers above named with the power of appointing assistants and subordinates in their respective departments. Said principal officers shall report to the Board at each stated meeting (and oftener when required) the operations of their respective departments during the recess, including appointments and removals, with a statement of the receipts and expenditures, purchases made, work and materials ordered, and the price therefor, and the supplies on hand; and at the annual meeting of the Stockholders they shall each submit a similar report of the operations of the year.

SECT. 5. The President, Treasurer, Secretary, and Superintendent of the Company shall be annually elected at the first meeting of the Board of Directors after their own election, or as soon thereafter as circumstances will permit.

The officers so elected shall hold their offices at the pleasure of the Board of Directors, and until their successors shall be duly chosen, unless sooner removed by the Board.

Vacancies caused by death, resignation, or otherwise, may be filled at any meeting of the Board, provided due notice thereof is given to the members prior to its meeting. All elections shall be by ballot, and a majority of the whole number of Directors for the time being shall be necessary to a choice. No person other than a Director shall be eligible to the office of President.

All persons owning and holding shares, either in their own right or as trustees, or as the legal representative of Shareholders, shall have a right to attend and vote at all meetings and elections of the Shareholders, and shall have as many votes as the number of shares so held or represented by them; but no person shall be admitted to vote at any such meeting or election as the proxy or attorney of any Shareholder, without a power of attorney duly executed.

SECT. 6. The salaries and compensation of the said principal officers shall be fixed annually by resolution of the Board, at its first meeting after the election of Directors, or as soon thereafter as is convenient; but such salaries may be changed at any stated meeting of the Board, if notice has been given of the intended change at the preceding stated meeting.

The salaries and compensation of all other employees of the Company shall be fixed by resolution of the Board.

SECT. 7. Before entering upon the duties of their respective offices, the Treasurer, the Superintendent, the Receiver, the Assistant Receiver, and any other officer or employee of the Company, from whom the Directors may see fit to require the same, shall each execute to the Company a bond—with one or more sureties, to be approved of by the Executive Committee—conditioned for the faithful performance of the duties of his office, including responsibility for negligence. The amount of the penalty of the bonds to be fixed by resolution of the Board.

SECT. 8. Except in the case of the President, no officer shall be a member of the Board of Directors, and the acceptance of an appointment by a Director shall be deemed a resignation of his seat at the Board; but a Director may, nevertheless, be designated to discharge the duties of an office temporarily, during a vacancy or disability.

SECT. 9. Subject to these By-Laws, and to such regulations and orders as the Board of Directors may from time to time make, the President shall have the chief management, control, and supervision of the affairs of the Company. It shall be his duty to preside at all meetings of the Board, to preserve order, to promote the regular and speedy transaction of business, and to attend the meetings of the Executive Committee.

All purchases, repairs and contracts, shall be made under his authority, except where otherwise provided by the Board; but he shall make no purchases and order no repairs not needful for the daily supplies and ordinary business of the road without the sanction of the Board of Directors, or, during their recess, of the Executive Committee.

He shall cause a book to be kept, in which all purchases and orders for repairs, work, or materials, with the prices, shall be recorded, and shall submit an abstract thereof to the Board at every stated meeting.

He shall appoint Conductors, Starters, Drivers, Storekeepers, and Stablemen, and may suspend or remove them; but, in all cases where the appointees are required to give security for the performance of their duties, the appointments shall not take effect until the Board of Directors or the Executive Committee shall have ratified them, and decided the security to be sufficient.

He shall keep a journal of all occurrences affecting the interests or business of the Company, and keep the Directors continually advised of the same; and he shall annually prepare, in time to be submitted to the Stockholders at the annual election, an account of the operations of the Company during the next preceding year, and a statement of the property and resources of the Company, its funded and floating debt (if any), outstanding contracts, and contingent liabilities.

He shall, either in person or by one of the principal officers, or one of the Directors designated for that purpose by him, visit or cause the depot and its appurtenances to be visited and inspected at least once in each week, and report or cause to be reported to the Board, at its next meeting thereafter, the result of such visits and inspections.

He shall have the power, in case of contemplated absence from the city or inability to attend to his official duties, to select from the Board of Directors one of its members to act as President *pro tempore* during the time of such absence or inability, which appointment shall be entered on the Book of Minutes of the Board; and in case of his inability or neglect to make such selection, the Board shall proceed, if in their judgment advisable, to elect a President *pro tempore* by ballot. An entry on the Book of Minutes shall also be made, showing the termination of such appointment.

The President *pro tempore* so selected shall be invested for the time being with all the powers and subject to all the requirements of the President herein before set forth, and shall receive for the period for which he shall perform such duties such compensation as the Board may prescribe.

SECT. 10. It shall be the duty of the Treasurer to receive all moneys belonging to the Company, and forthwith to deposit the same in a Bank, to be selected by resolution, to the joint credit of "The President and Treasurer of the Sixth Avenue Railroad Company," and the same shall only be drawn by the check of the Treasurer, countersigned by the President. He shall disburse all moneys directed or authorized to be paid by the Board; he shall keep true and accurate accounts and vouchers of all moneys received and disbursed; and no bill or account shall be paid by him unless certified by the President or Executive Committee, and such certificate filed therewith; he shall keep regular books of account of all moneys received and disbursed, which books shall be the property of the Company, and be delivered over with his papers and accounts to his successor, at the expiration of his term of office. He shall, at the annual meeting in each year, render an account of the financial condition of the Company, and of all items of money received and disbursed for the last year. He shall render an account at each stated meeting of the Board of Directors of the items and amounts of the receipts and expenditures for the preceding month. He shall also furnish from time to time such statements and accounts as shall be required by the Board of Directors, and shall, whenever so required, lay all books, papers, and accounts in his possessions, and relating to the business of the Company, before any meeting of the Directors or Shareholders.

Sect. 11. It shall be the duty of the Secretary to be in constant attendance during the office hours at the general office of the Company; to be present at the meetings of the Board; to keep full and perfect minutes of the proceedings, votes taken, resolutions adopted; to keep the books and records of the Company; and to give written or printed notice to all the Directors of the time and place of all the regular meetings and of all special meetings; and whenever any select committee shall be appointed in pursuance of a resolution of the Board, to furnish the chairman of the committee with a copy of the resolution, and the names of the members composing the committee. Whenever a resolution shall be adopted directing any duty to be performed by either of the officers of the Company, it shall be the duty of the Secretary to furnish, forthwith, notice thereof to such officer, with a copy of the resolution. When any vacancy in the Board of Directors is to be filled, or any of the officers particularly named in the fourth section of these By-Laws is to be elected, or any proposed amendment of the By-Laws to be acted upon, notification thereof shall be specially given in the notices of the meeting. A similar notification shall be made of the object of all special meetings.

The Secretary shall be the Registrar of all transfers of stock, and for that purpose he shall keep the accounts of the stock registered and transferred, in such form and manner, and under such regulations, as the Finance Committee or the Board shall from time to time prescribe. He shall obey all resolutions of the Board of Directors prescribing his powers and duties, and shall act under the orders of the President.

SECT. 12. The Superintendent shall have, subject to the direction of the President, the special superintendence of the track and cars, and the repairs and running of the road, and a general supervision of the depot, stables, and workshops, and over all the Conductors, Starters, Drivers, Hostlers, Mechanics, and Laborers in the Company's employ. And it shall be his duty to see that they are faithful to the interests of the Company. He shall endeavor, in all cases of persons leaving the employ of the Company, to obtain a settlement of their accounts, and a full discharge of all claims.

He shall furnish each Driver and Conductor with a printed copy of the regulations issued for their government, and shall see to the enforcement thereof. He may suspend Conductors, Drivers, Starters or Stablemen, for misconduct or incapacity, and report such suspension to the President, without delay.

In cases of accident, he shall—with all possible dispatch—ascertain and report to the President, in writing, the attendant circumstances, and the names and residences of witnesses.

He shall examine and certify the pay-rolls and bills for work done or purchases made by him, or under his supervision. In case he shall be authorized at any time to make sales of any property belonging to the Company, he shall make such sales for cash, and all moneys belonging to the Company, received by him, shall be paid over at once to the Treasurer. It shall be his duty to cause any purchase or sale he may be authorized by the Board of Directors, the President, or the Executive Committee to make, to be entered forthwith in the books kept by the Company for that purpose. It shall be his duty to see that the name of each Conductor, Collector, Starter, Mechanic, Driver and Laborer, shall be entered in the book kept by the Company for that purpose, with the date of the appointment or employment of each, and the amount of wages per day which he is to receive; and whenever any removal or suspension of any person appointed or employed shall be made, it shall be his duty to see that an entry thereof is forthwith made in such books. He shall, when required so to do, superintend the erection or repairs of the Company's buildings. He shall act as the general out-door agent of the Company in all matters specially intrusted to him by the President or Executive Committee, or by the vote of the Board of Directors; and at each stated meeting make a full written report, in detail, of his proceedings for the month ending on and including the Saturday preceding such meeting, with any information he may possess affecting the interests of the Company, or any changes which have taken place in the condition of its property under his supervision.

SECT. 13. It shall be the duty of the Deputy-Superintendent to keep the books of the Company, excepting those kept by the Treasurer and Secretary, to make out the pay-roll, and to see that the same shall be approved and certified by the Superintendent before any payments are made thereon. He shall obey all resolutions prescribing his powers and duties, and shall act under the orders of the President.

SECT. 14. The fiscal year of the Company shall commence on the first day of February, and end on and include the ensuing thirty-first day of January in each year.

SECT. 15. Dividends shall be declared semi-annually, providing the profits of the Company warrant the Board of Directors in declaring the same. It shall be the duty of the Treasurer to attend to the preparing of the account thereof, to pay out the same, and to take and preserve vouchers therefor in a book prepared for that purpose. Checks for dividends shall be made payable to the order of the parties entitled to receive the same.

SECT. 16. All transfers of the stock shall be made in the usual form, by the Stockholder signing in proper person or by attorney duly authorized, in a book provided for the purpose, a declaration of sale or transfer, setting forth the number of shares, the person to whom and the time when the same are transferred; and at the time of the transfer the old certificate shall in all cases be surrendered to the President, who shall see that the same is canceled, by writing across the face thereof a minute of the transfer, and of the numbers of the certificates issued in lieu thereof; and the said canceled certificate shall then be delivered to the Treasurer, and by him preserved. The Secretary shall report to the Executive Committee, at its stated meetings, the number and amount of shares of the certificates so surrendered since the last meeting, by whom given up, and the number and amount of shares for which new certificates have been issued in lieu thereof, and to whom. No transfer shall be made on the books of the Company for thirty days next previous to the annual election of Directors, nor for ten days next prior to the time appointed for the payment of any dividend. All certificates shall be issued and signed by the President and Secretary, and countersigned by the Treasurer, under such other regulations as the Board of Directors or Finance Committee may from time to time prescribe. No certificate shall be issued in place of one stated to be lost, unless by direction of the Board, on legal evidence of the loss and sufficient indemnity against loss to the Company.

SECT. 17. Deeds, contracts, and other legal documents, when authorized by the Board of Directors, shall be signed by the President and countersigned by the Secretary, and no officer shall sign or countersign any document in blank. Whenever any negotiable paper is issued by order of the Board of Directors in payment of the obligations of the Company, it shall be in the form of drafts drawn by the President upon the Company, payable to the order of the person entitled to the payment, and accepted by the Treasurer in behalf of the Company.

SECT. 18. These By-Laws may be amended by the Board of Directors at any meeting, by a vote of a majority of the whole number of the then existing Directors, provided notice of the motion to amend shall have been given at a previous stated meeting.

All previous By-Laws are hereby repealed.

ORGANIZATION

FOR CONDUCTING THE BUSINESS OF

THE WEST PHILADELPHIA PASSENGER RAILWAY COMPANY,

Adopted by the Board of Directors December, 1858.

That the duties, powers and responsibilities of the officers and employees of the West Philadelphia Passenger Railway Company may be defined and fully understood, and its accounts systematically kept, the Board of Directors have adopted the following organization for conducting the business of the road.:

The administrative duties upon the line of the road, its branches, and the connecting roads over which the Company's cars may hereafter pass, will be divided into the following departments, viz: The Transportation Department, Accounting Department and Treasury Department, with such other officers or agents for special objects as the Board may from time to time deem necessary. The whole to be under the general direction of the President, as the organ of the Board.

The Transportation Department will be committed to an officer, to be known as General Superintendent, who shall have charge of all the real estate and personal property of the Company on the line of their road, its branches and connections. To him will be entrusted the control and use of the road and branches, the motive power and appurtenances employed thereon, the shops, stables and depots, their machinery, tools, and materials, and the cars, whether upon their own road or upon connecting roads.

He will be held responsible for the regular and safe transportation of passengers and property over said road, and shall report from time to time as may be required by the President or Board, upon the condition of the road, its equipment, and the property connected with the road, and make such suggestions in relation to the same, as the business of the road, or their importance to him may dictate.

He shall have authority, with the assent of the President, to contract for materials for the repairs of the road, and buildings, but all important contracts, including iron rails, wooden stringers and ties, cars and horses, must be first sanctioned by the Board before being closed. Copies of all contracts must be furnished to the Secretary as soon as entered into.

All purchases for current supplies shall be made by the General Superintendent, to be subject to the approval of the Committee of Accounts, before they become binding upon the Company. A copy of the order given for these supplies shall be recorded in an Order Book, to be kept for that purpose. All accounts contracted during each month, with the bill of the articles furnished by the vendor at the time of delivery, must be handed to the Secretary, and by him, when approved by the Committee of Accounts, prepared for payment by the Treasurer.

Articles in constant and general use shall be kept in store at the Depot of the Company, under the general charge of the Superintendent, who may be assisted by a clerk, to be known as a Keeper of Stores, when in the opinion of the Board it may become necessary.

The General Superintendent shall be aided by two Dispatchers of Cars, one Stable Master, one Foreman of Track Repairs, and one Car Inspector, who shall perform the duties of their office in strict conformity to his directions.

The General Superintendent shall nominate, with the assent of the President, suitable persons for the offices of Dispatchers, Stable Master, Foreman of Track Repairs, Car Inspector and Conductors, in his department, and shall remove or suspend at his discretion, or by direction of the President or the Board, reporting in all cases to the Board the causes of dismissal.

The General Superintendent shall propose rules, defining the duties, in detail, of all his subordinate officers and agents, and submit the same to the Board of Directors for approval.

No officer shall be entitled to receive compensation until his appointment is confirmed by the Board, except when the appointment is temporary, or the person is taken on trial, which service shall not exceed a period of one month. The General Superintendent shall transmit to the Board, with each nomination, the testimonials or reasons that have induced him to make the appointment, and no new office shall be created by him without the assent of the Board of Directors. All books or papers in the possession of the General Superintendent or his subordinates, shall be open to the President, Directors, and Secretary. All moneys received by the General Superintendent shall be immediately paid over to the Treasurer, and a report of the amount, and the source from whence it was received, handed to the Secretary.

In case of accident upon the road, he shall immediately report the fact to the President, and institute a thorough investigation into the causes which led to it, the result of which shall be reported in writing to the Board.

The Secretary shall have charge of the Accounting Department. He shall record all office bills, and petty expenses of the office, when approved by the Board or Committee of Accounts, also all bills on special contracts, and bills for current supplies for the Transportation Department, and for the construction and equipment of the road, when the same have been approved by the Committee of Accounts, and shall charge them off, and enter them to their proper accounts, before handing them to the Treasurer for payment. He shall record all Pay Rolls, and charge off and enter them to their proper accounts, before being filed away by the Treasurer. He shall not enter any bill or claim unless certified by the proper officer, and approved by the Committee of Accounts; except for services paid for by Pay Rolls at established rates, and purchases by the General Superintendent, under authority of the Committee of Accounts.

The expense account shall be kept by him under the following heads, to be subdivided respectively, as follows, viz:

Construction and Equipment Account.
Conducting Transportation Account.

Construction and Equipment to include all expenses chargeable to capital stock account.

Conducting Transportation to include all expense connected with the working of the road, repairs of track, repairs of cars, repairs of buildings, and the keeping and maintaining the road, its fixtures and equipments in its original order for efficiency.

The items of each account shall be the following, viz:

CONSTRUCTION AND EQUIPMENT.

Right of Way.
Real Estate.
Buildings and Fixtures.
Graduation and Masonry.
Track and Fixtures.
Salaries of Officers.
Incidentals.
Cars.
Horses.
Harness.
Tools and Machinery.

CONDUCTING TRANSPORTATION.

Tools.
Iron Rails.
Wooden Stringers and Ties.
Frogs and Switches.
Chairs and Spikes.
Paving Materials.
Labor—Repairing Track.
Repairs of Cars.
Repairs of Buildings.
Rent and Furniture.
Gas.
Oil.
Fuel.
Horses.
Harness.
Feed.
Stable Labor and Expenses.
Watchmen.
Conductors.
Drivers.
Dispatchers and Assistants.
Taxes.
Stationery and Printing.
Salaries of Officers.
Incidentals.

The Secretary shall know that all officers and agents of the Company, whose duties require that they shall give bonds to the Company, have had the same properly made out and executed in legal form, and shall present them to the Board of Directors for approval, and after approved by the Board shall file them away in the General Office of the Company.

The Secretary shall keep a regular record of the proceedings of the Board of Directors of the Company; give notice to the members of all stated and special meetings, and shall attend the meetings of all standing or special committees when required.

He shall give at least twenty days notice of the annual meeting of the Stockholders, and ten days notice of any other general or special meetings of the Stockholders.

He shall receive from the Treasurer all old certificates of stock, immediately after their transfer, shall see that they have been canceled, and make a record of the same, and file them away in the general office of the Company.

He shall furnish the chairman of the Committee of Accounts, (whose duty it shall be to submit the same to the Board) on the Monday preceding the stated meeting in each month, a detailed statement of expenditures of the last current month, under their proper heads, as hereinbefore provided, and shall perform such other duties as the Board of Directors may require.

The Treasurer shall give bond, with one or more sureties, to be approved of by the Board of Directors, in the sum of not less than ten thousand dollars, nor more than twenty thousand dollars, for the faithful performance of all his duties.

He shall keep a regular set of books, containing the accounts of the Company, and of all the funds of the Company that may pass through his hands, and shall keep a separate account as Treasurer in such bank or banks as the Board of Directors may from time to time direct.

He shall on the Monday preceding each stated meeting of the Board, submit to the chairman of the Committee of Accounts, (whose duty it shall be to submit the same to the Board), a statement of the financial condition of the Company, as it stood on the last day of the preceding month, and at the stated meetings of January and July, of each year, a complete statement of his account for the six months previous, ending on the last days of June and December, of each year, and shall also prepare a full statement of the finances of the Company, to be submitted to the Stockholders at their annual meeting.

The Receiving Agents of the Company shall pay over their collections to the Treasurer, daily, or oftener if required to do so by the Board.

In all cases where the receipt of money is not otherwise provided for, the collections shall be made by the General Superintendent, and on its receipt by him, shall be immediately paid over to the Treasurer, and a memorandum of the same transmitted to the Secretary.

The Treasurer shall attend at the office of the Company during business hours, and whenever required, and shall take charge of all the funds of the Company, and make disbursements from the same, as directed by the Board of Directors.

He shall be entrusted with all the funds of the Company, and in connection with the President, issue and transfer its stock, bonds, or other securities, which may from time to time be authorized by the Board of Directors.

His books shall be open at all times to the inspection of the President or any member of the Board of Directors; all checks shall be signed by the President and countersigned by the Treasurer; all his office bills shall be approved by the Committee of Accounts, and endorsed to their proper account, and entered by the Secretary before being paid. All other bills before being paid by him, shall have been approved by the Committee of Accounts, and endorsed and entered to their proper account by the Secretary, except payments for services accounted for by Pay Roll, to which the receipts of the persons to whom it is due is attached, and cash purchases of the General Superintendent under special authority.

The accounts of the Treasurer shall be audited by the Committee of Accounts, or the chairman thereof.

All cases of defalcation, or any want of promptness or obedience on the part of any officer or agent of the Company, in making his returns to the Treasurer, shall be immediately reported by him to the President and to the Board of Directors.

There shall be appointed by the Board of Directors, two officers, to be denominated Receivers.

They shall be nominated by the President to the Board of Directors.

It shall be their duty to take from, and receipt to each Conductor, the amount of cash collected by him on each trip, to receive and record the number of tickets taken up which were issued by connecting roads, and to record such other evidences of indebtedness of other roads to this Company, as Conductors are required to report; and also report the same to the Treasurer, who shall make the necessary entries thereof in the books of the Company.

It shall be their duty to pay over to the Treasurer daily, all moneys received, and all evidences of indebtedness by connecting roads.

They shall keep a permanent record of the receipts per trip and per day of each Conductor, and shall perform such other duties, and keep such other records as the Board may from time to time direct.

The books shall be open to the inspection only of the President, the members of the Board of Directors, the Treasurer, Secretary, and the General Superintendent.

All persons connected with the Transportation Department, shall be under the supervision and direction of the General Superintendent, and those whose compensation consists of a stipulated fixed sum per day or month, shall devote their whole time to the services and interests of the Company, unless exempted therefrom by the Board of Directors.

All officers and agents who may by virtue of their office, receive money on account of the Company, shall give security for the faithful discharge of their duties, in such sums as shall be required by the Board of Directors, unless exempted therefrom by the Board of Directors.

All payments to regular employees of the Company shall be by Pay Roll, to which the veritable signature of the employee must be attached, and crosses or marks of those incapable of writing their name, must be witnessed.

All payments for purchases for current supplies, and for all expenses other than labor or services, shall be made on presentation of the bill to the Treasurer, certified by the proper officer, approved by the Committee of Accounts, and endorsed by the Secretary.

The Board shall fix the compensation of all officers and agents created by this organization, the wages of the subordinates shall be fixed by the head of the department, subject to the approval of the Board.

The appointment of all other employees, and the defining of their powers and duties, is vested in the General Superintendent, who shall be held responsible to the Board for the good conduct of all the employees in his department, and shall have the power of dismissal, when he thinks it for the interest of the Company, and shall report immediately the cause thereof to the Board.

In case of vacancy in the head of a department, the President shall make a temporary appointment to fill the va te meeting of the Board of Directors, which shall be valid until a permanent appointment is made by the Board.

No person addicted to the use of intoxicating drinks, or who is habitually vicious, profane, or uncivil in his deportment, shall be employed or continued in the service of this Company.

No officer or employee shall be permitted to be absent from the duties of his post, without the assent of the Board, the President, or the head of the department to which he belongs.

Free tickets shall be given by the President only, under general powers conferred by the Board.

The General Superintendent shall have power to issue passes to persons in the employ of the Company, when he thinks it to the interest of the Company to do so. All Conductors are prohibited from allowing any free travel, except on free tickets thus authorized.

AN ACT

RELATIVE TO THE CONSTRUCTION OF RAILROADS IN CITIES.

Passed April 4th, 1854.

The People of the State of New York represented in Senate and Assembly, do enact as follows:

SECT. 1. The Common Councils of the several cities of this State shall not hereafter permit to be constructed in either of the streets or avenues of the said city a railroad for the transportation of passengers which commences and ends in said city, without the consent of a majority in interest of the owners of property upon the streets in which said railroad is to be constructed being first had and obtained; for the purpose of determining what constitutes said majority in interest reference shall be had to the assessed value of the whole located upon such street or avenue.

SECT. 2. After such consent is obtained, it shall be lawful for the Common Council of the city in which such street or avenue is located to grant authority to construct and establish such railroad upon such terms, conditions and stipulations in relation thereto as such Common Council may see fit to prescribe. But no such grants shall be made, except to such person or persons as shall give adequate security to comply, in all respects, with the terms, conditions and stipulations so to be prescribed by such Common Council, and will agree to carry and convey passengers upon said railroad at the lowest rates of fare, nor shall such grants be made until public notices of intention to make the same, and of the terms, conditions and stipulations upon which it will be given, and inviting proposals therefor, at a specified time and place, shall be published under the direction of the Common Council in one or more of the principal newspapers published in the city in which such railroad is proposed to be authorized and constructed.

SECT. 3. This Act shall not be held to prevent the construction, extension or use of any railroad in any of the cities of this State which have already been constructed in part, but the respective parties and companies by whom such roads have been in part constructed, and their assigns, are hereby authorized to construct, complete, extend and use such roads in and through the streets and avenues designated in the respective grants, licenses, resolutions or contracts under which the same have been so, in part, constructed, and to that end the grants, licenses, and resolutions aforesaid are hereby confirmed.

AN ORDINANCE

TO REGULATE PASSENGER RAILWAYS.

SECT. 1. The Select and Common Councils of the City of Philadelphia do ordain, that all Passenger Railroad Companies within the city of Philadelphia shall be subject to the restrictions, limitations, terms and conditions hereinafter provided; and any such company, before entering upon any road, street, avenue or alley, within the limits of said city, shall be understood and deemed to be subject thereto, upon the conditions hereinafter prescribed.

SECT. 2. That it shall be the duty of said companies, or any of them, to conform to the surveys, regulations and gradients as they are now or may hereafter be established by law. They shall submit all proposed plans, courses, styles of rails, and the manner of laying the same, to the Board of Surveys and Regulations, for their approval and sanction, which shall be obtained before they proceed to break ground or occupy any of the highways as aforesaid; and they shall be further required to lay flag-stones or crossings along the line of the paved streets upon which the rails are laid, at intervals not exceeding two hundred and fifty feet; and any neglect, omission or refusal to do so on the part of any such company, shall be punishable by a fine of not less than fifty dollars for each and every offence, recoverable before any Alderman of the city of Philadelphia, and payable into the City Treasury.

SECT. 3. That all railroad companies, as aforesaid, shall be at the entire cost and expense of maintaining, paving, repairing and repaving that may be necessary upon any road, street, avenue or alley occupied by them. That for the convenience of the public, it shall also be the duty of such companies to clear the streets, or other public highways that they may occupy, of snow or any obstructions placed therein by such companies, when the same impedes the travel upon said highways, and for any neglect on their part to do so for a period of five days, they shall be punishable by a fine of twenty dollars for each square that may be so impeded, recoverable before any Alderman of the city of Philadelphia, and payable into the City Treasury, upon a complaint of five citizens residing therein, upon oath or affirmation: provided, nevertheless, that whenever any such company shall deem it inexpedient to use their said road during the continuance of the snow, they shall provide comfortable sleighs, or other suitable vehicles for the transportation of passengers along the route of their railway at the usual rates as aforesaid; then, and in that case, no such penalty shall be recoverable.

SECT. 4. That it shall be the duty of any Company, as aforesaid, when requested so to do by the Chief Commissioner of Highways, to remove any obstruction, mend or repair their road, pave or repave the highways, as herein before provided, and should they refuse or neglect to do so for ten days from the date of such notice, then and in such case the Councils may forbid the running of any car or cars upon the said road until the same is fully complied with; and the city reserves the right in all such cases to repair or repave such streets, and the expense thereof shall be a judgment upon the road, stock and effects of such Company, recoverable as judgments are now recoverable by the city of Philadelphia.

SECT. 5. It shall be the duty of said Company, or Companies, to employ careful, sober and prudent agents, conductors and drivers, to take charge of their car or cars when upon the road, and for the violation of any Act of Assembly, or Ordinance of the city, on the part of any such officer, or officers, or employees upon said road, the Company shall be liable to all fines, forfeitures or damages therefrom: provided, however, that this act shall not be taken to excuse or free any such officer or employee from the penalties or responsibilities of any such violations, or other acts by them committed.

SECT. 6. The running speed of the cars, upon any city Passenger Railroad, shall not at any time be at a greater rate than six miles an hour, in the paved and built-up portions of the city, nor shall they incommode the crossings, nor stop at the corners of any street or elsewhere, to solicit passengers. It shall also be the duty of conductors and drivers of the cars to give ample notice to drivers of vehicles and pedestrians of their approach, and also to afford all reasonable opportunity for them, or either of them, to avoid collision or accident; and any neglect by them to comply with the provision of this section shall be punished by a fine of five dollars, to be recovered before any Alderman of the city, and paid into the City Treasury, and the Mayor of the city is in such cases empowered to revoke the license of such car or cars, and they shall not be permitted to be again placed on the road until such license is renewed.

SECT. 7. It shall be incumbent on all Railroad Companies, as aforesaid, before placing cars upon their road, to pay into the office of the Chief Commissioner of Highways, and annually thereafter, for the use of the city, the sum of five dollars for each car intended to run on the same. They shall also have the number painted in some conspicuous place upon each car; and any omission, or neglect, to comply with either of these provisions, shall be punishable by a fine of ten dollars, to be recovered on complaint before any Alderman of the city, who shall pay the same forthwith into the City Treasury.

SECT. 8. The Directors of any such Company or Companies shall, immediately after the completion of any Passenger Railroad in the city, file, in the office of the City Solicitor, a detailed statement, under the seal of the Company, and certified under oath or affirmation by the President and Secretary, of the entire cost of the same; and the city of Philadelphia reserves the right any time to purchase the same, by paying the original cost of said road or roads, and cars, at a fair valuation. And any such Company or Companies refusing to consent to such purchase, shall thereby forfeit all privileges, rights and immunities they may have acquired in the use or possession of any of the highways as aforesaid; or should any such Company or corporation neglect to run cars upon their road or roads for the accommodation of the public, for the space of three consecutive months, the Councils reserve the right to rent the same to any other person or persons, company or companies, who will be willing to run cars on the same; or in the event of the Councils, as aforesaid, being unable to rent said road, or to place cars upon the same for one year after the same shall have been abandoned, as aforesaid, by the Company constructing or owning the same, then and in such case, the Councils reserve the right to cause the said road to be removed from the highways, and to sell or dispose of the materials thereof, and after paying all expenses arising therefrom, pay the balance, if any, to the legal representatives of the said defaulting Company.

SECT. 9. Any Passenger Railroad Company, which is now or may hereafter be incorporated in the city of Philadelphia, shall, by their proper officer or officers, who shall sign the same, file in the office of the City Solicitor a written obligation to comply with the provisions of this ordinance: provided, that no Railroad Company now incorporated shall be authorized to commence work upon any of the highways of the city until this section has been complied with; and a failure to do so for ten days shall be taken and deemed as a refusal on the part of such Company; and in case the Philadelphia and Delaware River Railroad Company should fail to comply with the provisions of this section, on or before the eighth of July, proximo, the City Councils hereby express their disapproval of an Act, entitled "A Supplement to an Act to incorporate the Philadelphia and Delaware River Railroad Company," approved June 9, 1857, which provides for the construction of a Passenger Railway, by a private corporation, over Fifth and Sixth streets, in the city of Philadelphia.

RULES AND REGULATIONS

To be observed on the several Street Railroads in the City of Boston, where Cars are drawn by Horses.

[Prescribed by the Mayor and Aldermen, June 27, 1857, and January 18, 1859.]

In the exercise of the rightful power reserved to this Board in the several and respective charters of the Metropolitan, Cambridge, Dorchester Avenue, Middlesex and Broadway Railroads, it is

Ordered, That the following rules shall be observed by the officers, agents and servants of the aforesaid corporations, in the mode of using the rails of their respective roads in the streets of Boston; and the same rules shall be applied to all other railroads which may hereafter be located in the streets of Boston.

First.—No car shall be drawn at a greater speed, in the city proper, in any street north of Dover street and the Federal street bridge, than five miles an hour, nor in any other street in the city, at a greater speed than seven miles an hour.

Second.—While the cars are turning the corners, from one street to another, the horses shall not be driven faster than a walk.

Third.—Cars driven in the same direction shall not approach each other within a distance of three hundred feet, except in case of accident, when it may be necessary to connect two cars together, and also, except at stations.

Fourth.—Cars running in different directions shall not be allowed to stop abreast each other, except at stations.

Fifth.—No car shall be allowed to stop on a cross walk, nor in front of an intersecting street, except to avoid collisions, or to prevent danger to persons in the street.

Sixth.—When the conductor of any car is required to stop at the intersection of two streets to receive or land passengers, the car shall be stopped so as to leave the rear platform slightly over the farther crossing.

Seventh.—The conductors and drivers of each car shall keep a vigilant watch for all teams, carriages, persons on foot, and especially children, either on the track or moving in the direction of the track; and on the first appearance of danger to such teams, carriages, persons or children, or other obstruction, the cars shall be stopped in the shortest time and space possible.

Eighth.—The conductors shall not allow ladies or children to enter or leave the cars while in motion. Other passengers may be allowed to enter the cars and depart therefrom, while the cars are at a full stop, or nearly stopped.

Ninth.—Conductors shall announce to the passengers the names of the squares and principal streets as the car reaches them.

Tenth.—Whenever there shall occur a fall of snow of sufficient depth to allow vehicles to pass over the same on runners, no snow plough shall be allowed to pass over the several tracks of the Street or Horse Railroad Corporations, within the limits of the City of Boston, nor shall the respective corporations cause or allow snow to be removed from their several tracks without consent being first obtained of the Superintendent of Streets, with the approbation of the Committee on Paving. The consent for the removal of the snow for the opening of the tracks being refused, the several corporations are authorized to use a sufficient number of sleighs to convey passengers requiring a transit over their respective roads, day by day, until the cars can be used on the tracks.

Eleventh.—The several corporations shall not sprinkle salt or any article of a decomposing nature on their tracks or rails, or cause or allow the same to be done by any of their agents, for the purpose of melting the snow; or wash, or cause to be washed by any of their agents, the said tracks and rails with brine or pickle, for a like purpose, unless a permit is granted by the Superintendent of Streets allowing the same to be done, and said permit shall only be granted when the use of said articles will not be detrimental to vehicles on runners crossing the tracks and rails.

Twelfth.—The several corporations shall place and keep placed, a printed copy of all the rules and regulations of the board of Aldermen, in a conspicuous position in each car run upon their respective roads.

AN ACT

CONCERNING THE ANNUAL RETURNS OF HORSE OR STREET RAILROADS IN THE COMMONWEALTH OF MASSACHUSETTS.

Be it enacted by the Senate and House of Representatives, in General Court assembled, and by the authority of the same, SECT. 1. That every horse or street railroad corporation that has been, or may be hereafter incorporated, shall, instead of the return now required from them by law, hereafter render to the Secretary of the Commonwealth, on or before the fifteenth day of October of each year, a return, that shall embrace full and complete information upon the several items hereafter enumerated.

CONDITION OF THE COMPANY.

Capital stock, fixed by charter.
Capital stock, as voted by the company.
Capital stock paid in, in cash.
Capital stock paid in, in work and materials, by contractors and others.
Funded debt.
Floating debt.
Total debt.
Amount of above debt secured by mortgage of the road and franchise, or any property belonging to the corporation, or standing in its name.
Number of mortgages on road and franchise, or any property of the corporation, specifying the number and amount of mortgages on road and franchise, and each kind of property.
Amount of assets on hand, exclusive of the road and equipment, and exclusive of all property on hand, used, or which is to be used, in running the road and keeping it in repair.

COST OF THE ROAD.

Amount expended for labor in excavating for the track, laying foundation, and rails.
Amount expended for timber for foundation.
Amount expended for iron and other metal for rails, chairs, spikes, or other articles, used in building the road.

Amount expended for paving.

Amount expended for paving stones.

Amount expended for engineering.

Amount expended for interest, salaries of officers during construction of road, and other expenses not included in any of the above items, which have been included on the books of the company in the cost of the road, not including items of equipment or running expenses as mentioned below.

Total cost of road.

Amount included in the present and in past years among the running expenses for estimated or actual depreciation of the road.

Net cost of road.

COST OF EQUIPMENT.

Number of cars, and cost.

Number of horses, and cost.

Cost of omnibuses, sleighs and other vehicles, excepting cars, owned by the company.

Cost of land and buildings thereon when purchased.

Cost of buildings used for offices, stables, &c., erected by the company, or standing on land not owned by the company.

Cost of other articles of equipment, specifying what.

Total cost of equipment.

Amount included in the present and in past years, in the running expenses, for estimated or actual depreciation of any of the above items.

Net amount at which the equipment stands charged on the books of the company.

CHARACTERISTICS OF THE ROAD.

Length of single main track.

Length of double main track.

Total length of road.

Length of branches owned by the company, stating whether they have a single or double track.

Aggregate length of switches, sidings, turnouts, and other track, excepting main track and branches.

Total length of rail.

Weight of rail used per yard, specifying whether of cast or rolled iron.

Maximum grade per mile on road, with length of grade.

Shortest radius of curvature, with length of curve,

Greatest length of single track on road between two turnouts.

Total length of main track which is paved.

DOINGS DURING THE YEAR.

Total number of miles run during the year.

Number of passengers carried in the cars.

Rate of speed adopted, including stops and detentions.

Rate of speed actually attained, including stops and detentions.

Number of persons employed regularly, specifying the occupations of each.

Total number of trips run during the year.

Average number of passengers each trip.

EXPENDITURES FOR WORKING THE ROAD.

For repairs of road, including repairs of foundation, renewals of iron and renewals of pavement.

For general repairs, including repairs of cars, omnibuses, and harnesses, and for shoeing horses.

For repairs of real estate, including repairs of buildings used as stables, offices, or for any other purposes, by the company.

For wages, including the wages of every person regularly employed, excepting the president, directors, superintendent and treasurer.

For interest.

For taxes and insurance.

For tolls paid other companies for the right to pass over their roads.

For rent paid other companies for use of their roads.

For provender—to include cost of hay, grain, straw, or other articles used for the food and bedding of horses.

For miscellaneous articles purchased during the year—such as harnesses, blankets, &c., the use of which continues for one or more years—and not included in the cost of equipment.

For loss of horses—that is to say, the difference between the present estimated value of the horses owned by the company subtracted from the estimated value of those on hand at the commencement of the year, added to the cost of those purchased during the year; or if this is the first report of the company, then the difference between the estimated value of the horses on hand and their cost—giving the present average estimated value of each horse.

For incidental expenses—to include printing, president, directors, treasurer and superintendent's salaries, and all expenses other than those belonging to the actual working of the road.

For all other expenses.

For amount charged on the company's books during the year for estimated or actual depreciation of the following property:—

Cars.
Horses.
Omnibuses.
Real Estate.
Road.
Other property.

EARNINGS.

Received from passengers in cars and omnibuses, and for tickets sold.
From other roads, as toll or rent for use of road.
From United States mails.
For sales of manure.
From other sources.
Total earnings.
Net earnings, after deducting expenses.
Surplus earnings of previous year on hand.
Net earnings as above.
Total surplus for payment of dividends.
Dividends declared during the year.
Total percentage of dividends for the year.
Present surplus.

MISCELLANEOUS.

Increase during the year—

Of capital stock as fixed by charter.
Of capital stock as voted by the company.
Of capital stock paid in.

Increase of funded debt, during the year.
Increase of floating debt, during the year.
Decrease of funded debt during the year.
Decrease of floating debt, during the year.
Increase of mortgage debt, during the year.

Decrease of mortgage debt, during the year.

Increase in cost of road, during the year, including amount charged for depreciation thereon.

Decrease in nominal cost of road by amount charged for depreciation thereon.

Increase in cost of equipment, during the year, including amount charged for depreciation thereon.

Decrease in cost of equipment by sale of any portion thereof, or by amount charged for depreciation.

List of accidents on road, during the year.

SECT. 2. All the returns required to be made by the first section of this act, shall be so made up as to include the business of the several companies therein named, for the year ending the thirtieth day of September preceding the time when the return shall be rendered to the Secretary of the Commonwealth, and all such returns shall be signed by a majority of the directors of the respective companies, and be sworn to, as the truth.

SECT 3. Every horse or street railroad corporatien that shall refuse or neglect to render the return required by the first and second sections of this act, shall forfeit and pay to the Commonwealth one hundred dollars for each and every day that they shall so refuse and neglect to make said return. And it is hereby made the duty of the Secretary of the Commonwealth to notify the attorney-general whenever any of the before-mentioned corporations shall refuse or neglect to make the returns required of them by this act, and it shall be the duty of the attorney-general to commence a suit in behalf of the Commonwealth at once, against said corporation, in any court competent to try the same, and to prosecute the same to final judgment.

SECT 4. It shall be the duty of the Secretary of the Commonwealth to cause to be prepared blank forms of returns, with spaces for the insertion of information upon the several items mentioned in the first section of this act, and transmit copies thereof to the several corporations mentioned in said first section.

SECT. 5. The second section of the acts of eighteen hundred and forty-nine, chapter one hundred and ninety-one, shall be so construed as to apply to all horse or street railway corporations that have been or may hereafter be established.

THE PHŒNIX IRON COMPANY,

SUCCESSORS TO

REEVES, BUCK & CO.,

MANUFACTURERS OF

Railroad Iron, Bar Iron, Car Axles,

HEAVY SHIP AND BRIDGE IRON, SPIKES, &c.

ALSO A SUPERIOR ARTICLE OF

WROUGHT IRON RAILROAD CHAIRS

With continuous lips, and made to fit exactly the flanges of Rails.

┴ AND L IRON, &C.

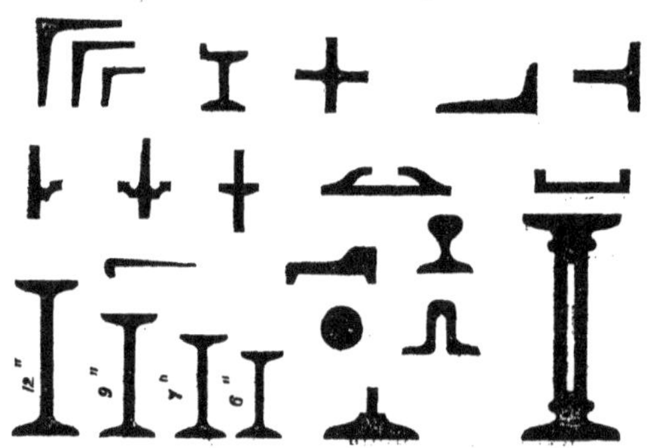

ALSO, WROUGHT IRON SOLID AND COMPOUND

GIRDERS & BEAMS

OF ANY REQUIRED LENGTH, FOR FIRE-PROOF BUILDINGS.

SAMUEL J. REEVES, V. Pres't,
No. 410 *Walnut Street, Philadelphia.*

AGENCY IN NEW YORK,
40 Exchange Place,
SAMUEL MILLIKEN, JR., Agt.

BURDEN'S HORSE & MULE SHOES,

MANUFACTURED AT THE

Troy Iron and Nail Factory,

H. BURDEN & SONS, Proprietors.

TROY, NEW YORK.

We are now manufacturing (upon Mr. H. BURDEN's improved and newly patented machinery,) and keep constantly on hand a full assortment of these Shoes, of the most approved form, and suited for heavy or light shoeing.

ECONOMY OF THE SHOES.

The saving by the use of these Shoes is not less than 50 per cent. The rapidity with which they are made, the small cost for attending the machine, its enormous capacity—one of them making thousands of tons a year—enable us to give an excellent article at a price but little above the cost of Horse Shoe Iron.

QUALITY OF THE IRON.

None but the best American Refined Iron is put into these Shoes, any of which will be found to bend double, cold, without breaking.

DURABILITY OF THE SHOE.

This is easily tested. Let any one shoe a horse on one side with "Burden's Shoes," and on the other with the best hand-made, of the same wearing surface and thickness, and he can judge for himself which he would prefer.

The thousands of horses used by the cavalry and artillery of the U. S. Army, and the still greater number of mules in the army transportation trains, are all shod with these shoes.

They can be purchased from the principal Iron and Hardware Stores throughout the United States, and from the subscribers.

They have been in use for a year past on many of the City Railway Lines in New York and Boston, and give entire satisfaction; among them are, and to whom we refer:

Sixth Avenue Railroad Co., New York,—WM. EBBITT, ESQ., Sup't.
Fourth Avenue Railroad Co., " } W. J. CAMPBELL, ESQ., Sup't.
Harlem Railroad Co., " }
Second Avenue Railroad Co., " } HUGHS, ESQ., Pres't. E. S. DICKERSON, ESQ., Sup't.
Middlesex Horse Railroad Co., Boston,—W. BONNEY, ESQ., Sup't.

We have all our different patterns lithographed, full size, with the weights marked on each, which we will forward by mail on application for same.

Address,

H. BURDEN & SONS,

TROY, NEW YORK.

POWELL & BROTHER,

ARCHITECTS, CIVIL ENGINEERS

AND SUPERINTENDENTS,

OFFICE, No. 69 Second Street, near Post Office,

And opposite the Town Clock,

W. ANGELO POWELL. **BALTIMORE, MD.**

We furnish Designs for every description of Buildings, in all the styles of Architecture, and make out accurate Estimates, Bills of Materials and quantities, Specifications, Contracts, Bonds, Detail Drawings and working full size details. Comprising complete Drawings, Plans, Elevations, Sections, Perspective Views, &c.

All Designs prepared with due regard to convenience, durability and economy in construction, and a guarantee not to exceed any specified estimate. All designs sent from this office, are accompanied with full and complete explanaations in every particular belonging thereto: such as

Public and Private Buildings of every kind, City and Country Churches, Ecclesiastical Structures, Chapels, Colleges, Infirmaries, Asylums, School Houses, Banks,

HOTELS, RAILROAD STATIONS,

Stores of Stone, Iron, &c., Halls of all kinds, Court Houses, &c. Also, Insurance Offices, IRON WORK, Patents, &c., Altars, Pulpits, Cemetery Entrances, &c., Cemeteries, Parks, Private Grounds, Fancy Walks surveyed, planned and laid out in the best manner; also, Towns surveyed and plotted, Maps & Surveys generally, Railways, &c.

Designs and Plans for Model Cottages, Suburban Residences, Villas, Farm Houses, Gate Lodges, Summer Houses, Fountains, Aviaries, and Arbors, Conservatories, &c.

Designs for Barns and Framing, Frame Work, Carriage Houses, Dwellings, Warehouses, Factories, **WOOD AND IRON BRIDGES.**

Also, every variety of designs for Monuments, Tomb Stones, Cenotaphs, Tablets, Sarcophagii, Vaults, Railings, &c.

We also attend to the furnishing of Iron Bridges complete,—ready for transportation, Castings, Girders, Railings, Verandas, Balconies, Lumber, &c., upon the best terms and principles.

In conclusion, we respectfully solicit a share of patronage, and promise to give satisfaction in all the branches. We have an experience of fifteen years in the business, and practical knowledge thereof, and have been engaged upon Government Works, Buildings, Bridges, and various important Edifices, as Architects, Civil Engineers and Superintendents. Prompt and personal attention will be given to all orders intrusted to us. Designs for Bridges, Stations, &c., will be sent to any part of the country with complete explanations.

JACOB BAILY,

IRON FOUNDER,

Corner Broad & Spring Garden Sts.,

PHILADELPHIA,

MANUFACTURER OF EVERY KIND OF IRON CASTINGS

Used in the construction of Street Railways;

HOUSE FRONTS, COLUMNS, &c.

Engineers from any part of the country may be supplied with Castings for Curves, Frogs and Switches, for any radius required.

THE SUBSCRIBER HAS ON HAND ALL THE PATTERNS NOW IN USE.

WOOD, MORRELL & CO.,

JOHNSTOWN,

CAMBRIA COUNTY, PENN'A,

MANUFACTURERS OF RAILROAD IRON

CHARLES E. SMITH & CO.,

FAIRMOUNT IRON WORKS,

Thirtieth Street, above Coates, Schuylkill,

(Address "BOX," Philadelphia P. O.) PHILADELPHIA, PA.,

Manufacturers of all sizes of Rails; old Rails Re-rolled; Street Rails; small Railroad Iron, suitable for turnouts, Warehouses, Coal Yards, &c. Also, Band Iron, Gas Tubing; T and L Iron; Marble and Stone Saws; Railroad Chair Iron, and Bands, and Bars, of extra width, length, or gauge; Punched Washers, of all regular sizes, kept constantly on hand. Any others made to order.

Chas. E. Smith. Stephen Morris. Chas. Wheeler, Jr. Stephen P. M. Tasker. Thos. T. Tasker, Jr.

LARGEST AND MOST EXTENSIVE

HARNESS AND TRUNK FACTORY

IN PHILADELPHIA,

At No. 720 Market St., (below Eighth.)

SALES ROOMS

CONTAIN

VERY LARGE ASSORTMENTS OF

Iron Frame, Steel Spring, Sole Leather

TRUNKS

AND TRAVELING BAGS,

Riding Saddles, Whips, &c.

E. P. MOYER & BROTHERS.

PASSENGER RAILROAD HARNESS

On hand and made to order at shortest notice, and WARRANTED good Leather and workmanship,

AT LOWEST CASH PRICES.

SAMUEL MACFERRAN,

IRON FOUNDER,

No. 532 ARCH STREET,

PHILADELPHIA,

Manufacturer of the Patent Frog for Street Railways.

STATE RIGHTS FOR SALE.

www.ingramcontent.com/pod-product-compliance
Lightning Source LLC
LaVergne TN
LVHW011233110826
845150LV00006B/1627

9781425514396